Lillard / Montessori: A Modern Approach

Montessori Today:
A Comprehensive Approach to Education from Birth to Adulthood
by Paula Polk Lillard

Dr. Montessori's Own Handbook:
A Short Guide to Her Ideas and Materials
by Maria Montessori

The Montessori Method
by Maria Montessori

MONTESSORI

A MODERN APPROACH

PAULA POLK LILLARD

SCHOCKEN BOOKS · NEW YORK

PHOTOGRAPHIC CREDITS

Richard Meyer: photographs 2, 7, 11, 12, 17, 19, taken at the
Winton Terrace Head Start Class, Cincinnati, Ohio; photo-
graphs 6, 8, 9, 16, 26, taken at the Xavier University Montessori
Class, Cincinnati, Ohio; photographs 4, 10, 13, 14, taken at
the Sands School, Cincinnati, Ohio; photographs 5, 15, 18, 20,
21, 23, taken at the Mercy Montessori Center, Cincinnati, Ohio.
James F. Brown: photographs 3, 24, 25, taken at the Xavier Uni-
versity Montessori Class, Cincinnati, Ohio.
Terry Armor: photographs 1, 22, taken at the Cincinnati Country
Day School, Cincinnati, Ohio.

Library of Congress Catalog Card Number 78-163334
ISBN 0-8052-0920-4

Manufactured in the United States of America

9

TO MY HUSBAND, JOHN,
for his encouragement and support, and to our daughters, Lisa, Lynn, Pamela, Angel, and Poppy, who made many sacrifices for "mother's paper."

THIS BOOK is not just a popular introduction in Montessori education. It is also that, of course: a well-chosen and coordinated presentation of its basic principles and techniques, preceded by a historical survey of its vicissitudes in the States and a preface giving a flash of a classroom at work, and ending with some considerations of its present-day value plus a perspective of ongoing research. As such, it offers to any educated person wishing to know what's what a condensed, all-around view of the whole field, based on reliable, well-documented information.

But its particular merit is its use for those working in the field of education and related sciences. No serious person thus engaged will deny the influence of Maria Montessori's ideas on modern thinking about the child and human development in general. The message of this woman must indeed have been forceful and profound to have had this kind of impact without losing its freshness up to the present day.

Mrs. Lillard has succeeded in bringing it over loud and clear for all who care to hear. She has not given in to the temptation of many authors writing on Montessori education—to give their own interpretation of it or to present its fundamental features together with ready-made criticisms. She lets, as it were, Maria Montessori speak for herself. The readers can draw their own conclusions.

Consequently, this book can be recommended as an introduction of Montessori's ideas to all professionals dealing with the human being. Parents and other educators should read it as a matter of course. It's the best in its class.

M. M. MONTESSORI

July 1973

Preface

In 1961, a close friend of mine gave me a book to read, entitled *Maria Montessori: Her Life and Work,* by E. M. Standing. I was most interested in the book because I knew my friend had determined her own children must have a Montessori education if at all possible. I did not remember ever having heard of Montessori before, although after reading Standing's book I think I must have read some of her work while majoring in education at Smith College. She was not popular at the time, but I'm certain I remember her ideas concerning playpens, children's sleeping hours, and several other ideas that impressed me and which I had followed in raising my own children.

Standing's book on Montessori did not impress me, however. It struck me as outdated, not very well organized, and offensive in its near deification of Montessori. More important, Montessori's description of the children in her schools seemed unrealistic to me. I had been a public school teacher, and I could not reconcile her accounts of children's behavior with my own experience. I dismissed Montessori as a turn-of-the-century Italian romantic, and felt some concern that my friend who had no background in education had been so impressed.

At this point, William Hopple, Assistant Headmaster of Cincinnati Country Day School, the private school that two of my children attended, visited the Whitby School in Greenwich, Connecticut. This school was founded by Nancy McCormick Rambusch in the late 1950's, and represents the initial re-introduction of Montessori to America. He was so impressed by what he saw that he came back to Cincinnati determined to begin a Montessori class for three- to six-year-olds in his own school.

Because of my respect for his judgment, I decided to take another look at Montessori—particularly with my three-year-old daughter in mind. I met Hilda Rothschild, the Montessori teacher who was to direct the class, and was favorably impressed by her. When Bill Hopple asked if I would serve as her assistant for the year, I agreed. My husband and I then entered our child in the class, feeling that, if something happened in the classroom we didn't approve of, we would know it immediately and could withdraw her. Like most parents, we are cautious when it comes to our own children!

What followed in the days ahead was beyond any imagining or expectation I could have had. There were sixteen three- and four-year-old children in the class, only four of whom were girls. They had not been pre-selected by the teacher; in fact, she had not seen them until the day school opened. Some of the children had special problems. Perhaps some of the parents who were interested in this class were looking to a new form of education for answers either to their children's problems or to inadequacies in themselves as parents.

What seemed so amazing to me that fall was the teacher's constant reaching out to the children, and the responses she aroused in them. She persistently called them away from aimless, destructive, sometimes chaotic behavior, and toward something in themselves that seemed to pull them together, to bring them into focus, and to free them for a constructive response to their world. Because of the personal integration they achieved, the atmosphere in the classroom was spontaneous, joyful, and purposeful. There was a peace and freedom from tension there that seemed to release the children to live their lives to the fullest.

The ways in which Mrs. Rothschild helped the children to create the unique environment in the classroom particularly impressed me. I should say, first of all, that she is an unusually wise and experienced teacher. Having trained under Dr. Montessori in France and taught in Montessori schools there, she fled to the United States when the Germans invaded France in World War II. In America, she became interested in special education, receiving a master's degree in this field from Syracuse University. She had taught a variety of classes for young children for twenty years before taking a refresher course in Montessori education in the United States, and becoming once again the teacher of a class recognized and defined as "Montessori."

Her approach to the children in the classroom could be summed up by one word—respect. She accorded to them the dignity, trust, and patience that would be given to someone embarked on the most serious of endeavors and who was, at the same time, endowed with the potential and desire to achieve his goal. There is much lip service, of course, paid in traditional education to the concept of respecting young children; yet it was obvious to me that what I was observing was something very different from anything I had seen before. This teacher seemed to have the knack of being inside a child's skin. She absolutely knew how deeply he had been hurt by some slight or how frustrated he felt when he was unable to make his needs known. Because she trusted his ability to tell her what was troubling him, she was constantly in a listening state. No matter how occupied she was with one individual child at a time, she was alert to the others. The antennae were always out. As one person observed after watching her class, "Why, that woman has eyes in the back of her head!"

She had an uncanny way of never letting herself get backed into a corner with children. No situation was allowed to deteriorate into a show of authority in the "It's you or me" sense—a battle the child must always lose and which causes him to lose some of his self-respect as well. She was a master of the light touch, and had a magical way of appealing to the imagination and love of drama in young children as well. She could close her eyes when the classroom seemed to border on the chaotic side, perhaps turn out the lights and stand as a statue caught in action, and either through silence or a whisper help the children to re-orient themselves so that they were both calmer and more alert to the world outside themselves.

As she struggled in those early weeks to help the children develop their potential for being in touch with themselves and involved with their environment in a meaningful way, she was often discouraged, and would express her concern to me. I, who was so amazed at how well things were going, couldn't imagine why she was so upset. By the end of the year I understood. While I thought things were going beautifully because the classroom was so superior to any of those I had ever seen, she had in mind where things were going—and that fall they were still a long way off. It really wasn't until two years later, when the oldest children had been in the class for three years, that it seemed to reach an optimal functioning. This seems obvious to me now, for I have seen the role the older Montessori children play in guiding, inspiring, and protecting the younger, but I was ignorant of this phenomenon at the time.

By spring of the first year, the children were happy and working hard. I knew then that this was an educational approach superior to any I had seen before, and that I wanted to support it. I did not know, however, if it was Montessori as a method that had impressed me or this particularly excellent teacher. Perhaps this was only her own interpretation, influenced as she had been by her work with crippled and retarded children, or by her twenty years of exposure to American children after her initial Montessori training. A method developed with European children fifty years earlier might have needed a good deal of interpretation in order to be suitable for American children in the mid-twentieth century. Was the classroom that inspired me really a Montessori classroom?

By chance, Helen Parkhurst, the teacher of the gold medal-winning Montessori classroom at the San Francisco World's Fair before World War I, was in Cincinnati in 1964. She was visiting a close friend, Miss Mary Johnston, with whom she had traveled to Italy to learn about Montessori's work in 1913. Miss Parkhurst had stayed on to become one of Montessori's most important teachers, and the woman Montessori entrusted to direct the introduction of her method to the United States in the years following the World's Fair. After an hour or so in the observation room, I asked her my question: "Was this a Montessori classroom?" Her answer was direct. "This is a Montessori classroom, and it is the best one I've seen in a long time." I knew then the approach to children I had so admired did indeed have a name, and that I wanted to direct my energies toward supporting and spreading this approach where I could.

I worked intensively for the next few years for Montessori programs in the Cincinnati community: a teacher-training program, Head Start classes, a public school class for graduates of Head Start, a six-year research program. I also saw other Montessori teachers and classes in the country, and became aware of the problems encountered when attempts are made to translate ideals into reality. I understand why many people find the Montessori classroom they happen to visit either too rigid or too permissive, depending on the teacher's personality, life style, or training. I can understand why John Holt (author of *How Children Fail*, and one of today's best-known educational writers) is concerned about the unevenness of quality in Montessori classrooms and the relative isolation of Montessori educators. In a letter to me in March of 1971, he wrote that he had seen Montessori schools he liked in places as diverse as Cincinnati, Ohio; Fort Worth, Texas; and Stamford, Connec-

ticut, but only last fall he had seen a Montessori class in
Indiana which was

> a most tense and anxious place in which the nun in charge
> defended everything she was doing by referring to Madame
> Montessori herself. The problem, of course, is one of "image,"
> as they say, and perhaps your book will do a great deal to
> change this. I remember saying when I spoke at the [American
> Montessori Society Convention] dinner five years ago that quite
> literally *all* of the people that I know who were interested in
> libertarian education expressed astonishment when I told them
> I was to speak at the Montessori convention. What was I doing
> with those people? Nothing much has happened since then to
> change this image. There is by now a very large movement in
> libertarian education with all sorts of publications, journals, etc.
> —a big communications network, so to speak. It would be easy
> enough for Montessori people to plug into this network and
> use it to speak their piece and clear up misunderstandings and
> misconceptions about their work, but it hasn't been done. I
> wonder how many Montessori schools know about the New
> Schools' Exchange Newsletter or are listed in their directory,
> or correspond with them at all. That would have been an ideal
> place for a running discussion in which some of these mis-
> understandings might have been cleared up. But perhaps you
> are the one, as I say, to lead Montessori educators out of what
> I would call their isolation . . .
>
> I suggested at the seminar that people consider dropping the
> label Montessori for their schools. I still think it is a good
> suggestion. There is something a little cultish about having a
> whole movement named after the founder—as in the case of
> the Rudolf Steiner schools. I think that most people have the
> impression of Montessori as of Steiner that they are rather
> esoteric and that they feel as if they have some sort of hammer-
> lock on the truth. To caricature it a little, something like:
> "What is all this fuss about education, we've known for years
> exactly what to do. All you have to do is follow us."

I hope all friends of Montessori will take the concerns of
Mr. Holt and others like him seriously, for I think the danger
of Montessori being misused and misunderstood in a number
of different ways is a real one in 1971. We know Montessori

identified hitherto-undefined qualities of child nature: principally, the construction by the child of his own inborn powers —a construction that takes place within him, hidden from our view, and yet whose process we can be alert to by careful observation of his outer actions; his uncompromising need, and therefore demand, for liberty; and his contribution to the wholeness of life as the "other pole of humanity." These we can defend. But unfortunately Montessorians, justified or not, have developed a reputation of being unwilling to accept the opportunity for growth that communication with others and open-mindedness to criticism provides. Edmund Holmes wrote in 1913,

> Orthodoxies—systems which have come under the patronage and control of the average man—are always wrong. When the Montessori heresy becomes an orthodoxy, the period of its decadence—as a system, not as a principle—will have begun . . . To regard as final the system which Dr. Montessori has elaborated would indeed argue a radical misunderstanding of her and of it.[1]

I hope this book, in which I have tried to put together in an organized way, and principally in her own words, the essence of Montessori, will inspire others to learn as much as they can about Montessori's contribution so that those who can will go beyond it. Dr. Montessori herself gave us the best advice to follow. In her concluding remarks at the Ninth International Montessori Congress in London, May 1951, she said, "The highest honor and the deepest gratitude you can pay me is to turn your attention from me in the direction in which I am pointing—The Child." [2]

Acknowledgments

I AM MOST GRATEFUL for the generous help and advice of Mrs. Hilda Rothschild and the Graduate School staff of Xavier University and in particular to Martha McDermott of Xavier and Sister Mary Jacinta of the Mercy Montessori Center for their help with Chapter 5. I am also indebted to Mildred Montgomery and the parents of the children in the Sands School and West End Presbyterian Church Montessori classes for the comments on Montessori they contributed to Chapter 6. Without the encouragement and support of Barbara Finberg of Carnegie Corporation of New York and John Holt this book would not have been written, and I owe special thanks to them. I am most appreciative to Judith Elliott for the fine typing and secretarial help, and to Edith Williams, who helped me to keep my household going during these busy months.

Contents

By education must be understood the active help given to the normal expansion of the life of the child.
—Maria Montessori, THE MONTESSORI METHOD, p. 104

Scientific observation then has established that education is not what the teacher gives; education is a natural process spontaneously carried out by the human individual, and is acquired not by listening to words but by experiences upon the environment.
—Maria Montessori, EDUCATION FOR A NEW WORLD, p. 3

A section of photographs
begins on page 91

1

Historical Introduction to Montessori

Maria Montessori was born in the province of Ancona, Italy, in 1870. When she was three, her parents moved to Rome in order that their only daughter might receive a better education. They encouraged her to become a teacher, the only career open to women at the time. However, Montessori was a women's liberationist before her time, and was determined not to accept a traditional woman's role. She was first interested in mathematics, and decided on a career in engineering. She attended classes at a technical school for boys, but eventually became interested in biology, and finally determined to enter medical school. Her struggles for admission are not recorded, except that she was first refused, and subsequently accepted, earning scholarships each year and tutoring privately to pay for a large portion of her expenses. This was important, as her father highly disapproved of her chosen career, and financial independence was necessary in order for her to continue her studies.

In 1896 she became the first woman to graduate from the University of Rome Medical School, and joined the staff of the university's Psychiatric Clinic. As part of her duties there, she visited the children committed to the general insane asylums in Rome. She became convinced that these mentally deficient children could profit from special education, and travelled to London and Paris to study the work of two earlier pioneers in this field, Jean Itard and Edouard Séguin.

Upon her return, the Italian Minister of Education asked Montessori to give a course of lectures to the teachers of Rome. This course developed into the State Orthophrenic School, and Montessori was named its director in 1898.

She worked with the children there for two years, basing her educational methods on the insights she had gained from Itard and Séguin. All day, from 8:00 A.M. to 7:00 P.M., she taught in the school, and then worked far into the night preparing new materials, making notes and observations, and reflecting on her work. These two years she regarded as her "true degree" in education.[1] To her amazement, she found these children could learn many things that had seemed impossible. She wrote,

> I succeeded in teaching a number of the idiots from the asylums both to read and to write so well that I was able to present them at a public school for an examination together with normal children. And they passed the examination successfully. . . . While everyone was admiring the progress of my idiots, I was searching for the reasons which could keep the happy healthy children of the common schools on so low a plane that they could be equalled in tests of intelligence by my unfortunate pupils![2]
>
> I became convinced that similar methods applied to normal children would develop or set free their personality in a marvelous and surprising way.[3]

This conviction led Montessori to devote her energies to the field of education for the remainder of her life.

To prepare for her new role as an educator, Dr. Montessori returned to the University of Rome to study philosophy, psychology, and anthropology. She made a more thorough study of Itard and Séguin, translating their writings into Italian, and copying them by hand. "I chose to do this by hand," Montessori wrote, "in order that I might have time to weigh the sense of each word, and to read, in truth, the *spirit* of the author." [4] During this time she also made a special study of nervous diseases of children, and published the results of her researches in technical journals. In addition, she served on the staff of the Women's Training College in Rome (one of the two women's colleges in Italy at that time), practiced in the clinics and hospitals in Rome, and carried on a private practice of her own.

In 1904, she was appointed Professor of Anthropology at the university, and carried on her other activities as well until 1907, when her active life as an educator began. She was asked to direct a day-care center in a housing project in the slum section of San Lorenzo, Italy. Montessori accepted, seeing this as her opportunity to begin her work with normal children. She was to have the care of sixty children between the ages of three and seven while their illiterate parents were working. Because of her other duties, she acted in the capacity of a supervisor to the project, hiring a young servant girl to serve as the teacher.

Montessori described her pupils as

tearful, frightened children, so shy that it was impossible to get them to speak; their faces were expressionless, with bewildered eyes as though they had never seen anything in their lives. They were indeed poor, abandoned children who had grown up . . . with nothing to stimulate their minds.[5]

A simple, bare room was provided for the children in an apartment building of the project. The sparse furniture was similar to that used in an office or home, and the only educational equipment was the pieces of sensorial apparatus Montessori had used with her mentally defective children.

Montessori says she had no special system of instruction she wished to test at this point. She wanted only to compare the reactions of normal children to her special equipment with those of her mental defectives, and in particular to see if the reactions of younger children of normal intelligence were similar to those of chronologically older but retarded children. She did not structure the environment for a scientific experiment. She stated that the artificial conditions required for scientific experiments would prove a great strain on her children, and would not reveal their true reactions. Instead, she attempted to set up as natural an environment as possible for the children, and then relied on her own observations of what occurred. She considered a natural environment for the child to be one where everything is suitable for his age and growth, where possible obstacles to his development are removed, and where he is provided with the means to exercise his growing faculties. After instructing the teacher in the use of the sensorial apparatus, she remained in the background, and waited for the children to reveal themselves to her. That they would, in fact, do so, she had no doubts. She believed that the young child is

at a period of creation and expansion, and it is enough to open the door. Indeed that which he is creating, which from not being is passing into existence, and from potentiality to actuality, at the moment it comes forth from nothing cannot be complicated . . . and there can be no difficulty in its manifestation. Thus by preparing a free environment, an environment suited to this moment of life, natural manifestation of the child's psyche and hence revelation of his secret should come about spontaneously.[6]

What happened next, Montessori says, brought her a series of surprises which left her "amazed and often incredulous." The children showed a degree of concentration in working with the apparatus which was not observable in the mentally deficient children at the Institute, and which seemed astonishing in children so young. Even more astonishing, the children seemed to be not only rested, but satisfied and happy after their concentrated efforts:

It took time for me to convince myself that this was not an

illusion. After each new experience proving such a truth, I said to myself, "I won't believe yet, I'll believe it next time." Thus for a long time I remained incredulous and, at the same time deeply stirred.[7]

The pattern that led to this phenomenon was each time observed to be the same. First, the child would begin to use a piece of apparatus in the accustomed way. But, instead of putting the equipment away when the exercise had been completed, the child would begin to repeat it. He would show "no progress in speed or skill; it was a kind of perpetual motion." [8] One child was observed to repeat such an exercise forty-two times, and to be concentrating so deeply that she was oblivious to deliberate attempts to disturb her, including picking her up in her chair and moving her to another part of the room. Suddenly, for no apparent reason, she was finished with her task and put the equipment away. But "what was finished and why?" questioned Montessori, and why should the children actually be rested and appear to have "experienced some great joy" after such a cycle of activity? [9]

A second surprising phenomenon in the children's behavior occurred quite by accident. The teacher was accustomed to distribute the materials to the children. However, one day she forgot to lock the cupboard where the equipment was kept. She arrived at the classroom to find that the children had already chosen what pieces they wished for themselves, and were busily at work. Montessori interpreted the incident as a sign that the children now knew the uses of the materials, and wanted to make their own choice. She instructed the teacher to let them do this, and constructed low shelves so the materials would be more accessible to them. She noticed that they consistently left some of the materials unused. She removed them, reasoning that the ones chosen must represent to them some particular need or interest, and that the others would only create confusion. She was quite surprised to notice that the "toys" she had placed in the room were among those things virtually untouched. These she also eventually removed.

Other unexpected phenomena occurred. The children seemed indifferent to rewards or punishments related to their work. They would, in fact, often refuse a reward or give it away. They showed an intense interest in copying the silence of a baby brought to class one day. From this experience, Montessori developed an "exercise of silence." It consisted of controlling all movements and listening to the sounds of the environment. The children's enjoyment in this group effort seemed to reflect some need for communication with each other and the world about them. The fact that these young children possessed a deep sense of personal dignity also became apparent. One day, they were so pleased at being shown how to blow their noses, they burst into applause! Eventually the children began to demonstrate a newly developed self-possession. They greeted visitors, who were now coming in ever-increasing numbers to see the classroom, warmly and respectfully. They seemed proud of their work and happy to show it to them. They demonstrated a sense of community and concern for each other. But it was the discipline, concentrated attention, and spontaneity of the children, evident in the peaceful atmosphere of the classroom, that most impressed visitors. Montessori says, "This could never have come about if someone like a teacher teaching by word of mouth had called forth their energies from the outside." [10]

There was one startling development of more direct academic significance. Montessori had not intended to expose children so small to any activity bearing on writing and reading. However, their illiterate mothers began to beg her to do so. She finally gave the four- and five-year-olds some sandpaper letters to manipulate, and trace over with their fingers. The children were quite enthusiastic about the letters and would march about the room with them, as if they were banners. Some eventually began to connect sounds with the letters, and to try to sound out and put together words. Soon, they had taught themselves to write. In a burst of activity they began to write everywhere. They would read the words they had written, but were uninterested in those anyone else had written. It was another six months before they seemed to understand what it is to read words. They then began to read with the same enthusiasm that they had written, reading every extraneous item in their environment—street signs, signs in shops, etc. They showed little interest in books, however, until one day a child showed the other children a torn page from a book. He announced there was a "story on it," and read it to the others. It was then that they seemed to understand the meaning of books.

They began reading them with the explosion of energy they had previously exhibited in writing and reading words encountered at random in their environment. The process was interesting on three counts: one, the spontaneity and direction of this activity from the beginning belonged to the children; two, the usual process, of reading preceding writing, was reversed; three, the children involved were only four and five years of age.

In observing all these developments in the children, Montessori felt she had identified significant and hitherto unknown facts about children's behavior. She also knew that, in order to consider these developments as representing universal truths, she must study them under different conditions and be able to reproduce them. In this spirit, a second school was opened in San Lorenzo that same year, a third in Milan, and a fourth in Rome in 1908, the latter for children of well-to-do parents. By 1909, all of Italian Switzerland began using Montessori's methods in their orphan asylums and children's homes.

In these schools, Montessori found a significant and consistent difference in the initial response of children from wealthy homes and those of poor families. The children of the poor, generally, responded immediately to the equipment offered them. The children who had intelligent and loving parents to watch over them and had been saturated with elaborate toys typically took a few days to a number of weeks to pay any real attention to the materials offered. However, once an intense interest was aroused in these children, phenomena began to appear similar to those seen in the first Casa dei Bambini. First, the children's cycle of repetition, concentration, and satisfaction would begin. It would lead to a development of inner discipline, self-assurance, and preference for purposeful activity. Montessori called this process which took place in the child "normalization." It appeared to her, in fact, to be the normal state of the child, since it developed spontaneously when the environment offered the necessary means.

Word of Montessori's work spread rapidly. Visitors from all over the world arrived at the Montessori schools to verify with their own eyes the reports of these "remarkable children." Montessori began a life of world travel—establishing schools and teacher training centers, lecturing, and writing. The first comprehensive account of her work, *The Montessori Method*, was published in 1909. In 1929, she could write,

> There is not one of the great continents in which [Montessori] schools have not been distributed—in Asia from Syria to the Indies, in China and in Japan; in Africa from Egypt and Morocco in the north to Cape Town in the extreme south; the two Americas: in the United States and Canada, and in Latin America.[11]

Montessori made her first visit to the United States for a brief lecture tour in 1912. She was given an enthusiastic welcome, including a reception at the White House. She gave her first lecture at Carnegie Hall to overflowing crowds, and stayed at the homes of such famous people as Thomas Edison, who admired her work. An American Montessori association was formed with Mrs. Alexander Graham Bell as President and Miss Margaret Wilson, President Woodrow Wilson's daughter, as Secretary. So pleased was Montessori with her reception here she returned in 1915, this time to give a training course in California. During this visit a Montessori class was set up at the San Francisco World's Fair and received much attention.

Montessori schools were started all over the country, one of the first being established in Alexander Graham Bell's home. A flood of articles on Montessori education appeared in the popular press and educational journals. However, this initial burst of enthusiasm for Montessori gradually met with an equal torrent of criticism by those American professionals who espoused the established psychological and educational theories of the period. Most influential of these was the noted professor William Kilpatrick. In 1914, he published a book, *The Montessori System Examined*, in which he dismissed Montessori techniques as outdated. Kilpatrick's book is important in the history of Montessori in the United States, not only because it is credited as the strongest single influence in dissolving the enthusiasm that had greeted Montessori in this country, but also because some of the areas of disagreement it outlined are the principal ones still being advanced. Kilpatrick himself was a man to be reckoned with in the educational world. A leading exponent of John Dewey's philosophy, he was a popular and respected professor at Teacher's College, Columbia University. Whatever he had to say was likely to have a profound impact on his fellow professionals. He addressed his small volume on Montessori to public school teachers and superintendents because he said they were

concerned to know the meaning of this agitation. . . . They are critical, if not skeptical. . . . They are tolerant enough of new dogma and experiment, [but they] would weigh every item of the idealistic projects of radicals, and even of the practical successes of experiments born among the differing conditions of foreign soil.[12]

Professor Kilpatrick based his evaluation of Montessori on her first book, *The Montessori Method*, which had just been published, and on an investigating trip to Rome to visit classrooms there. In addition, he had a private interview with Dr. Montessori.

Her theories viewing the child's nature as essentially good and education as a process of unfolding what has been given the child at birth, her belief in liberty as an essential ingredient for this unfolding, and her utilization of sense experiences in this process of development, he saw as "containing a greater or less amount of truth," but needing "to be strictly revised in order to square with present conceptions." [13] Further, due to the fact that one of the primary influences on Montessori's work was Séguin, a man whose work was first published in 1846, and that she "still holds to the discarded doctrine of formal or general discipline," Kilpatrick wrote, "we feel compelled to say that in the content of her doctrine, she belongs essentially to the mid-nineteenth century, some fifty years behind the present development of educational theory." [14]

Kilpatrick focused his criticism of Montessori on two areas: the social life of the classroom and the Montessori curriculum. There was a tidal wave in the early 1900's pushing American thought toward viewing the school primarily as a place not for individuals to acquire intellectual knowledge, as had been true in the past, but for them to develop social life and action. There was a "world-wide demand that the school shall function more definitely as a social institution." [15] Kilpatrick criticized Montessori because

> she does not provide situations for more adequate social cooperation.[16]
>
> The Montessori child, each at his chosen task, works, as stated, in relative isolation, his nearest neighbors possibly looking on. [He] learns self-reliance by free choice in relative isolation from the directress. He learns in an individualistic fashion to respect the rights of his neighbors. . . . It is thus clearly evident that in the Montessori school the individual child has unusually free rein.[17]

In contrast to this individualistic approach, Kilpatrick would "put the children into such a socially conditioned environment that they will of themselves spontaneously unite into larger or smaller groups to work out their life impulses as these exist on the childish plane." [18]

Kilpatrick was extremely critical of the materials Montessori constructed for the children's use in the classroom. He considered them inadequate, because he found little variety in them and because their aim was not sufficiently social.

> The didactic apparatus which forms the principal means of activity in the Montessori school affords singularly little variety [and] by its very theory presents a limited series of exactly distinct and very precise activities, formal in character and very remote from social interests and connections. So narrow and limited a range of activity cannot go far in satisfying the normal child. . . . The best current thought and practice in America would make constructive and imitative play, socially conditioned, the foundation and principal constituent of the program for children of kindergarten age.[19]

He also found fault with the materials because he felt they did not stimulate the child's imagination sufficiently. "On the whole, the imagination, whether of constructive play or of the more aesthetic sort is but little utilized" in the Montessori curriculum, and therefore it "affords very inadequate expression to a large portion of child nature." [20]

Although agreeing with Montessori's concept of "auto-education," Kilpatrick found it "more a wish than a fact" in her method because

> it is too intimately bound up with the manipulation of the didactic apparatus. . . . Life itself and situations that arise therefrom [give] abundant instances of evident self-education. . . . The nearer the conditions to normal life that the school can be brought, the more will real problems present themselves naturally (and not artificially at the say-so of the teacher). At the same

time, the practical situation which sets the problem will test the child's proposed solution. This is life's auto-education.[21]

Kilpatrick was particularly critical of the sensorial materials in the Montessori curriculum. "The didactic apparatus—the most striking feature of the system to the popular mind —was devised to make possible a proper training of the senses." [22] He then went on to dismiss this concept of training the sensorial powers because "the old notion of the existence of faculties of the mind and their consequent general training is now entirely rejected by competent psychologists. We no longer speak of judgment as a general power of observation." [23] Whatever is necessary in terms of "concepts, such as hardness, of heat, or of weight, etc., come in the normally rich experience of the child life; and conversely those that do not so come are not then necessary." [24] The Montessori doctrine of sense training

is based on an outworn and cast-off psychological theory. . . . The didactic apparatus devised to carry this theory into effect is insofar worthless . . . What little value remains to the apparatus could be better got from the sense experience incidental to properly directed play with wisely chosen but less expensive and more childlike playthings.[25]

Kilpatrick had a "difficult interview" with Montessori because the interpreter was not versed in psychology, but he "came away convinced that Madame Montessori had up to that time not so much as heard of the controversy on general transfer." [26]

Kilpatrick ended his examination of the Montessori curriculum with a discussion of her academic materials, specifically her approach to writing, reading, and arithmetic. First, he found it unnecessary to begin the foundation for these activities as early as three or four, as in Montessori practice. Therefore, it was not important to discuss how these skills might be presented to the child under six. At the end of the sixth year it was sufficient that the child

> should have a certain use of the mother tongue . . . reasonable skill, using scissors, paste, a pencil or crayon and colors. If he is able to stand in line, march in step, and skip, so much the better. He should know enjoyable games and songs and some of the popular stories suited to his age. He should be able, within reason, to wait on himself in the matter of bathing, dressing, etc. Propriety of conduct of an elementary sort is expected.
>
> Does any one question that knowledge and skill such as this can be gained incidentally in play by any healthy child? Indeed, so satisfied have many parents been of this point that they believe a kindergarten course unnecessary, feeling that home life suffices. Without accepting such a position, we may ask whether a group of normal children playing freely with a few well-chosen toys under the watchful eye of a wise and sympathetic young woman would not only acquire all this knowledge and skill and more, but at the same time enjoy themselves hugely? Surely, to ask the question is to answer it.[27]

For her efforts in mathematical apparatus, Kilpatrick found "there is little to be said. About the only novelty is the use of the so-called long stair. . . . On the whole, the arithmetic work seemed good, but not remarkable; probably not equal to the better work done in this country." [28] As to Montessori's approach to reading, he found its phonetic basis unsuitable to the English language.

> Any attempt to meet these difficulties could but result in a plan identical with one or another of the quasi-phonetic methods familiar enough to American primary teachers. It thus turns out that the Montessori method of teaching reading has nothing of novelty in it for America.[29]
>
> The appraisal of Madame Montessori's contribution in the case of writing is difficult. On the whole, it appears probable she has in fact made a contribution. Of how much value this can prove to those who use the English language is uncertain. Probably experimentation only can decide.[30]

He closed his discussion of the academic materials by agreeing "with those who would still exclude these formal school arts from the kindergarten period," not because it is difficult for a six-year-old to learn to read and write,

> but that the presence of these tends to divert the attention of parent, teacher, and child from other, and for the time, possibly more valuable parts of education. Education is life; it must presume first-hand contact with real vital situations. The danger in the early use of books is that they lead so easily to the monopoly of set tasks foreign to child nature, lead so almost inevitably to artificial situations devoid alike of interest and vital contact. An unthinking public mistakes the sign for the reality, and demands formulation where it should ask experience; demands the book where it should ask life.[31]

The one area of Montessori materials Kilpatrick regarded favorably were the practical life exercises. He saw them as having "immediate utility" and meeting "an actual and immediate social demand" such as cooking food for meals, taking care of the school environment, etc.[32]

Kilpatrick concluded his book with a comparative discussion of Montessori and Dewey. He found

> the two have many things in common. Both have organized experimental schools; both have emphasized the freedom, self-activity, and self-education of the child; both have made large use of "practical life" activities. In a word, the two are cooperative tendencies in opposing intrenched traditionalism.

He saw wide differences, however, in that Montessori "provides a set of mechanically simple devices" which "in large measure do the teaching." She could do this because she held "to an untenable theory as to the value of formal systematic sense training." Montessori also "centered much of her effort upon devising more satisfactory methods of teaching reading and writing." Dewey, on the other hand, "while recognizing the duty of the school to teach these acts, feels that early emphasis should be placed upon activities more vital to child life which should at the same time lead toward the mastery of our complex social environment." [33] Kilpatrick stated that Dewey's

> conception of the nature of the thinking process, together with his doctrine of interest and of education as life,—not simply a preparation for life,—include all that is valid in Madame Montessori's doctrine of liberty and sense training and, besides, go vastly farther in the construction of educational method.

Kilpatrick finished his book by saying "they are ill advised who put Madame Montessori among the significant contributors to educational theory. Stimulating she is; a contributor to our theory, hardly, if at all." [34]

The tremendous outpouring of energy that had created such a startling beginning for Montessori in America peaked soon after the publication of Kilpatrick's book, and subsided as rapidly as it had begun. By 1918, there were only sporadic references to Montessori in the journals. During the years 1916–18, Montessori herself travelled between Spain, where she was directing the Seminari Laboratori di Pedagogia at Barcelona, and the United States. After this time she did not return to the United States. The dismissal of Montessori as insignificant and outdated by Kilpatrick and others stood virtually unchallenged in America for over forty years. This American phenomenon of boom and bust was unique. Except for the temporary closing of Montessori schools in countries taken over by the Nazi and Fascist regimes, Montessori continued to flourish in other parts of the world without interruption. Much of this activity today is directed by the Association Montessori Internationale with headquarters in Amsterdam.

Montessori was appointed Government Inspector of Schools in Italy in 1922. However, she was increasingly exploited by the Fascist regime, and by 1931 she had begun to work chiefly out of Barcelona. Montessori made her last visit to Italy in 1934 for the Fourth International Montessori Congress in Rome. In 1936 revolution broke out in Barcelona, and she established permanent residence in the Netherlands. Her work was interrupted in 1939 when she went to India to give a six-month training course, and was interned there as an Italian national for the duration of World War II. She established many schools in India, however, and today it is an active Montessori center. Montessori died in the Netherlands in 1952, receiving in her later years honorary degrees and tributes for her work throughout the world.

It was five years after her death that an American renaissance for Montessori education began. It was accomplished initially by the single-minded determination and energy of Nancy Rambusch, a young American mother who became interested in Montessori during her travels in Europe. After receiving her Montessori teacher training and certification from the Association Montessori Internationale, she founded a Montessori class in New York. This class later became the Whitby School in Greenwich, Connecticut. Mrs. Rambusch lectured extensively to American educators and parents, and this time the climate was right. Over one thousand Montessori schools are now established in the United States, and the number increases rapidly each year.

What had happened in America in those forty years that caused alert professionals and laymen alike to reconsider the contribution of Montessori? Two major factors appear responsible. First, America was a disenchanted land educationally in the late 1950's. For a decade Dewey's theories and practices supposedly held sway in the classroom. How expertly these were carried out by the convinced, or how stubbornly they were resisted by unbelievers, are questions well worth considering. The point remains, however, that Americans—particularly parents—were alarmed by the results of our educational system. A significant number of children couldn't read above the most rudimentary level after twelve years of schooling. Too many students were choosing the first opportunity to drop out of school, even though it meant they were giving up any hope of ultimately making their own way in our ever more complex society. Perhaps worst of all, excellent students were betraying their individuality and the development of whatever unique talents they might possess to play the "school game." They were functioning like computers: experts at absorbing what the teacher put forth, sorting out what she wanted back, and regurgitating it in the manner in which she most liked to receive it. Americans were clearly alarmed by these phenomena. In addition, Sputnik had startled a nation accustomed to feeling smugly superior in the field of scientific technology. A kind of panic swept over the land, and in their fear many people took a closer look at the educational system they had counted on to insure their safety through advances in scientific knowledge and superior weaponry. The growth of population and aspirations for college careers had also created tremendous competition for entrance to good schools, colleges, and universities across the country. This, too, meant that many parents were taking a serious look at the education of their children for the first time in a decade. Americans were not only receptive to new ideas and approaches in education when Nancy Rambusch began her promotion of Montessori in the United States; they were actively seeking them.

A second factor involving the reception of Montessori in the 1950's was the gradual evolution that had taken place in the conceptual framework of American culture, particularly in regard to psychology and education. All through the 1940's and 1950's, post-Darwinian influences, the Freudian impact, the accepted theories of motivation, of the brain's operation, and of the maturation and growth of the child were being gradually absorbed and reconstructed. This re-thinking was sparked in large measure by dramatic new discoveries in the laboratories of psychologists and physiologists. Most important for our purposes here, these discoveries began to substantiate, one after another, the very Montessori theories and practices which had been so dissonant with previously accepted educational and psychological theories. It is interesting that Montessori herself felt it would be through the sciences that her newly identified needs of the child would be recognized. In 1917, she wrote,

> It is obvious that a real experimental science, which shall guide education and deliver the child from slavery, is not yet born; when it appears, it will be to the so-called "sciences" that have sprung up in connection with the diseases of martyred childhood as chemistry to alchemy, and as positive medicine to the empirical medicine of bygone centuries.[35]

The four areas of Montessori education that had been most out of step with the theories of the early 1900's involved the Montessori emphasis on intellectual or cognitive development, sensory training, the sensitive periods of the child's growth, and the child's spontaneous interest in learning. Cognitive development had always been a primary concern of educators. However, Freud's discoveries of the emotional and sexual development of the human being, and its influence on his behavior throughout his life, had had a stunning impact on the American educational scene. Progressive thinkers and educators were for the first time recognizing the instinctual drives and needs of the child. It was perhaps inevitable that there would be an extreme swing away from intellectual development and toward an attempt to deal directly in the classroom with these newly recognized phenomena. Impressed by Freud's discovery of the havoc that repressed hostility and desires can play, educators and parents adopted a somewhat permissive attitude toward behavior that had previously not been tolerated. Even physically destructive behavior was sometimes accepted. It was felt to be good for children to punch dolls, beat clay, knock over blocks and toys, and bang things in order to work out their repressions. (I am referring to such behavior in the home or school environment, and not in the therapy situation.) It is only recently that many parents have become aware that their permissiveness and lack of limit-setting in this and other areas has led to undisciplined, unhappy children.

Montessori felt that physically abusive behavior in children was destructive. Far from making the child feel better about himself, she observed that it left him more dissatisfied than ever. She did not permit such behavior in the classroom, feeling it was not a part of real freedom. She emphasized in its place the child's ability to discover himself, and his capacities for a positive response to his environment through the joy of discovery and creative work. She believed a lowering of standards of conduct or intellectual development would only lead to an inferior education and society.

> If education is to be an aid to civilization, it cannot be carried out by emptying the schools of knowledge, of character, of discipline, of social harmony, and, above all, of freedom.[36]

Darwin's theory of evolution based on natural selection had left the American culture of the early 1900's with a belief in fixed intelligence. Montessori's emphasis on early cognitive development was clearly out of step with this concept. Why be concerned about cognitive development if intelligence is a constant, not subject to significant modification? The accepted theory of predetermined development was also a heritage from Darwinian influence. If the human embryo follows the evolution of the species in its development, later growth, including mental development, might well proceed in predetermined stages that occur regardless of outside influences. Arnold Gesell is familiar as the foremost describer of these stages in the child's growth. The resulting child-rearing approach was one of "letting the child outgrow it" whenever unpleasant behavior appeared. As one father said to me, "My son [now eighteen] has been going through 'a stage' since he was two years old!"

Montessori believed that the child must have certain conditions in his environment or he will not develop normally; and, further, when periods of disruptive behavior occur, it is because the child is trying to tell us that some great need of his is not being met. His reaction is often violent because he is literally fighting for his life. She found this type of behavior disappeared when the child began to concentrate on his work, and, thereby, developed self-confidence and self-acceptance through the discovery of himself and his capacities.

Both the belief in fixed intelligence and the theory of predetermined development were dealt a death blow in the 1940's when American psychologists began to turn their attention to the effects of early environmental conditions on the mental development of children. Freud's discoveries had stimulated interest in infancy and early childhood in the early 1900's. The emphasis, however, was on emotional, not intellectual, development. After World War II, emphasis on the young child's cognitive development began to flourish as well. Children in orphanages and institutions were discovered to be suffering from severe retardation. This occurred in spite of the fact that the children had been given good to excellent physical care. In one such institution, sixty per cent of the children two years old could not sit up alone; eighty-five per cent of those four years old could not walk. One consistent observation was made about these institutions: there was little or no sensory stimulation for these infants. The walls were colorless, there was little sound, there was next to no activity to observe. Apparently the paucity of sensory stimuli in the early environment did have an effect on the development of these children. Psychologists began to design experiments to discover the effects of sensorial deprivation in other settings. One of these psychologists was Donald Hebb, a man whose work and thinking have significantly altered the course of contemporary American psychology. Experimenting first with rats and then with dogs, Hebb found that the richness of their early environment varied their adult problem-solving ability considerably. In 1949 Hebb published his *Organization of Behavior,* a book theorizing on his laboratory work. This book provided the first psycho-theoretical base for Montessori's approach to early learning and environmental stimulation. Before this time the brain was thought to operate through simple stimulus-response patterns or connections. These connections were conceived to be developed by repeated experiences and associations and to become permanent mental fixtures. The brain's functioning was likened to a telephone switchboard. (It was on this hitherto accepted concept of the brain's structure and operation that Kilpatrick had based his rejection of the transfer-of-learning theory, and, therefore, one of his major objections to Montessori education.) This theory of the brain's operation could not adequately account for the phenomena Hebb and others were finding in the laboratory in regard to early environmental influence on intellectual development. Hebb developed a much more complex theory of the neurological structure and processes of the brain which did consider these phenomena. He maintained that in early learning "cell assemblies" representing images or ideas are formed, and that in later learning these assemblies are joined into "phase sequences" which facilitate more complex thinking. Thus later learning would depend on the richness of the earlier formed cell assemblies.

Montessori's observation of the child's spontaneous interest in learning also received support from Hebb's theorizing. Previously all behavior was believed to be motivated solely by instinctual or homeostatic needs (the desire of the organism for a balanced physical and chemical state). If this were true, organisms would be quiescent if no such motivation was present. On the contrary, physiologists had recently established that the central nervous system is continuously active regardless of outer or organic stimulation. Hebb theorized that there must be an intrinsic motivation for behavior in addition to the already recognized motivation based on instinctual drives and homeostatic needs. Some of the important work supporting this new theory was done by H. F. Harlow. In three separate studies, he found that monkeys can and do learn to work puzzles when no motivation has been offered other than the presentation of the puzzle itself. It was demonstrated that real learning had taken place as, once the puzzle had been mastered, it was worked flawlessly and persistently. Harlow even demonstrated that the use of hunger-reducing rewards actually destroyed motivation, rather than supporting it. He found that monkeys who had been rewarded with food for working their puzzles ignored them as soon as they were finished. The unrewarded monkeys, on the other hand, often continued to explore and manipulate the puzzle after they had completed it.[37] Almost fifty years earlier, by observing children directly, rather than animals in the laboratory, Montessori came to similar conclusions concerning the inner motivation of children toward learning. She had established a classroom procedure based on this inner motivation, wholly discarding the gold stars, special privileges, grades, etc., which are still common practice in classrooms today as inducements to learning.

J. McVicker Hunt is another pioneer in the field of motivational learning who is particularly pertinent to Montessori. He observed that infants develop recognition patterns and will act to reproduce them (crying to seek mother's return) after six months of age. Gradually the infant also becomes interested and finds pleasure in novelty within a recognized context, and will actively seek it. "A major source of pleasure resides in encountering something new within the framework of the familiar." [38] Novelty becomes a source of motivation, then, if there is the right correspondence of the old with the new.

That novelty that is attractive appears to be an optimum of discrepancy in this relationship between the informational input of the moment and the information already stored in the cerebrum from previous encounters with similar situations.[39]

If there is too much novelty or incongruity, the child will be overwhelmed; if there is too little, he will be bored. Hunt called the dilemma of finding the right amount of each for any particular child at a given moment in time "the problem of the match." He gave Montessori credit for being the first educator to solve this problem on a practical level through giving the child freedom of choice in selecting from a wide variety of materials, graded in difficulty and complexity.

In addition to the work of American psychologists, others were making discoveries in early learning and cognitive development important to the acceptance of Montessori education. Although his work is just now receiving wide recognition in this country, Jean Piaget, the Swiss psychologist, had been at work in this field since the 1930's. Unlike most American psychologists of this time, Piaget worked directly with children to develop his understanding and theories. Because this was also Montessori's method, it may account for the many similarities in their beliefs. One area in which they closely parallel involves the role of sensori-motor training in the child's cognitive development. As early as 1942, Piaget wrote,

> Sensori-motor intelligence lies at the source of thought, and continues to affect it throughout life through perceptions and practical sets. . . . The role of perception in the most highly developed thought cannot be neglected, as it is by some writers.[40]

This, of course, is Montessori's view of sensory perception, a view not shared by other educators in 1912, including the influential Kilpatrick. Piaget's theorizing concerning the child's achievement of this pre-verbal intelligence is reminiscent of Montessori's description of the Absorbent Mind.

> The real problem is not to locate the first appearance of intelligence but rather to understand the mechanism of this progression. . . . One of us [Piaget] has argued that this mechanism consists in *assimilation* (comparable to biological assimilation in

the broad sense): meaning that reality data are treated or modified in such a way as to become incorporated into the structure of the subject.[41]

Piaget sees the child's thought as developing in progressive stages: from the beginnings of perception to symbolic thought to concrete operations and, finally, to the beginnings of formal thought in pre-adolescence. Piaget's stages are thus consistent with Montessori's theory and practice of leading the child through concrete experiences to progressively more abstract levels. One phenomenon in this procedure which so amazed Montessori is beautifully described by Piaget: that of the repetition which takes place when the child is establishing his basis for moving into abstract thought.

The development of thought will thus at first be marked by the repetition, in accordance with a vast system of loosenings and separations, of the development which seemed to have been completed at the sensori-motor level, before it spreads over a field which is infinitely wider in space and more flexible in time, to arrive finally at operational structures.[42]

Montessori's emphasis on sensitive periods in the child's life also is compatible with Piaget's theory of the development of the child's intelligence. Piaget saw the mental development of the child as a succession of stages or periods, each extending and building out of the previous one. During each period, new cognitive structures are formed and integrated out of the old.

These overall structures are integrative and non-interchangeable. Each results from the preceding one, integrating it as a subordinate structure, and prepares for the subsequent one, into which it is sooner or later itself integrated.[43]

If the opportunity for developing the needed structures in any given period is missed, the child's subsequent growth will be permanently impeded. Freud had suggested the concept of sensitive periods in the development of children as early as 1905. However, it was in 1935, almost thirty years later, that Konrad Lorenz produced the first laboratory research documenting their existence. He designed an experiment involving the imprinting phenomena in the social behavior of birds. Geese in one group were allowed to remain with their parents after hatching. A second group was removed from their parents immediately upon hatching, and Lorenz presented himself to them as a parent substitute. The first group reacted to other geese later in life in the expected ways of the species. The second group, however, behaved throughout their lives as if human beings were their natural species. Lorenz concluded that species recognition was imprinted upon the nervous system of the young geese immediately upon their hatching. Imprinting has been the subject of numerous experiments and studies since 1950, and, as a result, sensitive periods in early human development are now generally accepted.[44]

Piaget's work sheds light on two areas of Montessori often misunderstood: the development of the social and affective characteristics of the child and the growth of his creativity. Montessori had found that these developed spontaneously as the child's intelligence became established through his interaction with a prepared environment. This was an indirect approach to these areas, in contrast to the more direct approach of traditional education. Piaget presents a theoretical base that would tend to support Montessori's indirect approach. In his theory, the child begins his life "entirely centered on his own body and action in an egocentrism as total as it is unconscious (for lack of consciousness of the self)." Through his cognitive development, he begins "a kind of general decentering process whereby the child eventually comes to regard himself as an object among others in a universe that is made up of permanent objects." [45] It is this cognitive aspect of the developmental processes that makes possible the child's affective and social development. This process of decentering begins at approximately eighteen months and culminates in adolescence.

It has long been thought that the affective changes characteristic of adolescence, beginning between the ages of twelve and fifteen, are to be explained primarily by innate and quasi instinctive mechanisms. This is assumed by psychoanalysts who base their interpretation of these stages of development on the hypothesis of a "new version of the Oedipus complex." In reality, the role of social factors (in the twofold sense of socialization and cultural transmission) is far more important and is favored more than was suspected by the intellectual transformations we have been discussing.[46]

The development of creativity also depends upon the child's progression through the stages of cognitive growth: from sensori-motor intelligence to intuitive thought to concrete operations and, finally, formal operations. In intuitive thought, the child can evoke absent objects in his mind, a process necessary for creative thought, but they are in effect "stills" of moving reality. The child has an internal map of reality, but it is filled with blank spaces and insufficient coordinations. In concrete operations, the child is no longer dependent on the form of absent objects in his thinking, but he is still dependent on his understanding of the reality behind them. When the child reaches that stage of cognitive development where formal operations are possible, "there is even more than reality involved, since the world of the possible becomes available for construction and since thought becomes free from the real world."[47] Creativity then is not developed by a concentration on its stimulation, so much as it evolves at the end of a long process of cognitive development which had absorption of reality as its beginning point.

Montessori's concept of the interdependent relationship of cognitive development and artistic expression is now shared by men in the arts as well as psychologists. Rudolf Arnheim,

Professor of the Psychology of Art at Harvard University, in a recent book entitled *Visual Thinking*, states:

> artistic activity is a form of reasoning, in which perceiving and thinking are indivisibly intertwined. A person who paints, writes, composes, dances . . . thinks with his senses. . . . Genuine art work requires organization which involves many and perhaps all of the cognitive operations known from theoretical thinking.[48]

Arnheim finds fault with our educational system which has separated the development of reason and sense perception. In education the child studies numbers and words; the arts are presented to him as entertainment and mental release. Arnheim believes the arts have been neglected because they are based on sensory perception. It is apparent from the earlier rejection of Montessori's emphasis on sensory training that the development of perception has been neglected in traditional education. Arnheim calls for a re-emphasis on the importance of perception in the education of the child's mental powers. "My contention is that the cognitive operations called thinking are not the privilege of mental processes above and beyond perception, but the essential ingredients of perception itself." [49] Educationally, this means presenting the young child with "pure shapes," objects "of a wide variety of clearly expressed shape, size and color." [50] Arnheim credits the Montessori method as the first educational approach introducing children to the perceptual properties of pure quantities through such shapes. It may have been Montessori's background as a scientist that led to her unusual approach to creativity in children, for Arnheim sees art and science as closely related and requiring similar powers in man.

> Both art and science are bent on the understanding of the forces that shape existence, and both call for an unselfish dedication to what is. Neither of them can tolerate capricious subjectivity because both are subject to the criteria of truth. Both require precision, order, and discipline because no comprehensible statement can be made without these.[51]

This discussion has shown that Montessori philosophy and method are very much in step with the latest psychological and educational theories. The importance of early environmental conditions in the child's mental development, the role of sensory perception, the intrinsic motivation of the child, the sensitive periods in the child's development, and the role of cognitive development in the establishment of the social and creative powers of the child are all now recognized.

One last and crucial area dealing with the acceptance of Montessori in America today remains: reception by teachers. Although it appears better today than in 1914, it is still a very real problem. The type of person who has gone into teaching in the past has too often been one who has a need to control other human beings. Such a person will feel threatened by the Montessori approach, which puts the child in control of his own learning. The fate of Montessori education in America will largely depend on the ability of young men and women, whether already teachers or not, to develop the humility, wisdom, and flexibility required for the indirect teaching approach of Montessori.

2

The Montessori Philosophy

MONTESSORI DEVELOPED a new philosophy of education based upon her intuitive observations of children. This philosophy was in the tradition of Jean Jacques Rousseau, Johann Heinrich Pestalozzi, and Friedrich Froebel, who had emphasized the innate potential of the child and his ability to develop in environmental conditions of freedom and love. Educational philosophies of the past, however, did not emphasize the existence of childhood as an entity in itself, essential to the wholeness of human life, nor did they discuss the unusual self-construction of the child Montessori had witnessed in her classrooms. Montessori believed that childhood is not merely a stage to be passed through on the way to adulthood, but is "the other pole of humanity." [1] She considered the adult to be dependent on the child, even as the child is dependent on the adult.

> We ought not to consider the child and the adult merely as successive phases in the individual's life. We ought rather to look upon them as two different forms of human life, going on at the same time, and exerting upon one another a reciprocal influence.[2]

Montessori regarded the child as "a great external grace which enters the family" and exercises "a formative influence on the adult world." [3]

We are aware of the dependency of the child on the adult in our culture. We do not so readily recognize the dependency of adults on children in our fast-paced, adult-centered society. Montessori regarded this negligence as a tragic mistake leading to much of our unhappiness, greed, and self-destruction. In 1948 she stated her

> conviction that humanity can hope for a solution of its problems, the most urgent of which are those of peace and unity, only by turning its attention and energies to the discovery of the child and the development of the great potentialities of the human personality in the course of its construction.[4]

To explain the child's self-construction, Montessori concluded he must possess within him, before birth, a pattern for his psychic unfolding. She referred to this inborn, psychic entity of the child as a "spiritual embryo." This spiritual embryo is comparable to the original fertilized cell of the body. This cell does not contain the adult form in miniature, but rather a predetermined plan for its development. In a similar way, the child's psychic growth is guided by a predetermined pattern, not visible at birth.

Montessori believed this psychic pattern is revealed only through the process of development. For this process to occur, two conditions are necessary. First, the child is dependent upon an integral relationship with his environment, both the things and the people within it. Only through this interaction can he come to an understanding of himself and the limits of his universe and thus achieve an integration of his personality. Second, the child requires freedom. If he has been given the key to his own personality and is governed by his own laws of development, he is in possession of very sensitive and unique powers which can only come forth through freedom. If either of these two conditions are not met, the psychic life of the child will not reach its potential development, and the child's personality will be stunted. Since this pattern exists in the child and is operating even before birth, Montessori determined that education, too, "should start as early as the birth of the child." [5]

Montessori considered the dependent relationship of the child's psychic growth to free interaction with his environment a natural result of his mental and physical unity. Western educational thought had been influenced by Descartes' view of man as divided into two parts, the intellectual and the physical. Montessori now challenged this philosophical position, and stated that the full development of psychic powers is not possible without physical activity.

One of the greatest mistakes of our day is to think of movement by itself, as something apart from the higher functions. . . . Mental development *must* be connected with movement and be dependent on it. It is vital that educational theory and practice should become informed by this idea.[6]

If movement is curtailed, the child's personality and sense of well-being is threatened. "Movement is a part of man's very personality, and nothing can take its place. The man who does not move is injured in his very being and is an outcast from life." [7]

Through her observations of the child, Montessori became convinced that he possesses an intense motivation toward his own self-construction. The full development of himself is his unique, and ultimate, goal in life. He spontaneously seeks to achieve this goal through an understanding of his environment. "He is born with the psychology of world conquest." [8] His emotional and physical health will literally depend upon this constant attempt to become himself. Montessori pointed out that this goal was not for the self-centered purposes often found in contemporary culture. She wrote in 1949, "Today's principles and ideas are too much set on self-perfection and self-realization." [9] The goal of self-development is rather for service to mankind as well as individual happiness.[10]

Although the child has a predetermined psychic pattern to guide his striving for maturity, and a vital urge to achieve it, he does not inherit already established models of behavior which guarantee him success. Unlike other creatures of the earth, he must develop his own powers for reacting to life. He has, however, been given special "creative sensitivities" to help him accomplish this difficult task. These inner sensitivities enable him to choose from his complex environment what is suitable and necessary for his growth. The whole psychic life of the child rests upon the foundation these sensitivities make possible. A delay in their awakening will result in an imperfect relationship between the child and his environment. "Not feeling attraction, but revulsion, he fails to develop what is called 'love for the environment' from which he should gain his independence by a series of conquests over it." [11]

These transient faculties or aids exist only in childhood, and give no evidence of their existence in the same form and intensity much after the age of six. Montessori considered them proof that a child's psychic development does not take place by chance, but by design. She identified two such internal aids to the child's development: the Sensitive Periods and the Absorbent Mind.

Sensitive Periods are blocks of time in a child's life when he is absorbed with one characteristic of his environment to the exclusion of all others. They appear in the individual as "an intense interest for repeating certain actions at length, for no obvious reason, until—because of this repetition—a fresh function suddenly appears with explosive force." [12] The special interior vitality and joy the child exhibits during these periods result from his intense desire to make contact with his world. It is a love of his environment that compels him to this contact. This love is not an emotional reaction, but an intellectual and spiritual desire.

If the child is prevented from following the interest of any given Sensitive Period, the opportunity for a natural conquest is lost forever. He loses his special sensitivity and desire in this area, with a disturbing effect on his psychic development and maturity. Therefore, the opportunity for development in his Sensitive Periods must not be left to chance. As soon as one appears, the child must be assisted. The adult

> has not to help the baby to form itself, for this is nature's task, but he must show a delicate respect for its manifestations, providing it with what it needs for its making and cannot procure for itself. In short, the adult must continue to provide a suitable environment for the psychic embryo, just as nature, in the guise of the mother, provided a suitable environment for the physical embryo.[13]

Montessori observed Sensitive Periods in the child's life connected with a need for order in the environment, the use of the hand and tongue, the development of walking, a fascination with minute and detailed objects, and a time of intense social interest.

Order is the first Sensitive Period to appear. It is manifested early in the first year of life, even in the first months, and continues through the second year. It is important to understand that Montessori saw a clear distinction between the child's love of order and consistency, and the mature adult's milder pleasure and satisfaction in having everything in place. The child's love of order is based on a vital need for a precise and determined environment. Only in such an environment can the child categorize his perceptions, and thus form an inner conceptual framework with which to understand and deal with his world. It is not objects in place that he is identifying through his special sensitivity to order, but the relationship between objects. He has an

> inner sense which is a sense not of distinction between things, so that it perceives an environment as a whole with interdependent parts. Only in such an environment, known as a whole, is it possible for the child to orient himself and to act with

purpose; without it he would have no basis on which to build his perception of relationship.[14]

The child manifests his need for order to us in three ways: he shows a positive joy in seeing things in their accustomed place; he often has tantrums when they are not; and, when he can do so himself, he will insist on putting things back in their place.

A second Sensitive Period appears as a desire to explore the environment with tongue and hands. Through taste and touch, the child absorbs the qualities of the objects in his environment and seeks to act upon them. Equally important, it is through this sensory and motor activity that the neurological structures are developed for language. Montessori concluded, therefore, that the tongue, which man uses for speaking, and the hands, which he employs for work, are more intimately connected with his intelligence than any other parts of the body. She referred to them as the "instruments" of man's intelligence.

The child must be exposed to language during this Sensitive Period or it will not develop. Perhaps the most poignant description of such a happening is Itard's account of the "wild boy" of Aveyron. Abandoned in the forests of France as an infant, the child was found in young manhood, probably still in his teens. Covered with scars from his wilderness survival, his movements and behavior were those of an animal. Itard was able to help this boy develop his potential for human life in almost all ways. However, the boy did not develop language, even though it was established that the boy was not deaf and no other defect obstructing lingual development could be found.

The child in our culture is usually surrounded by the sounds he needs in establishing language. The use of his hands during this Sensitive Period is often another matter, although it is equally essential to his development. He must have objects to explore in order to develop his neurological structures for perceiving and thinking, just as he must be exposed to the world of human sound in order to develop his neurological structures for language. During this period the child is usually surrounded by adult objects. "The command 'Don't touch!' is the only answer to this vital problem of infant development. If the child touches such forbidden objects, he is punished or scolded." [15] It is also important to remember that the child's actions are not due to random choice, but directed by his inner needs for development. "Now the child's movements are not due to chance. He is building up the necessary co-ordinations for organized movements directed by his ego, which commands from within." [16] Therefore, it is of the utmost importance that the adult be guided by tolerance and wisdom when placing any necessary limits on the child's need to touch and taste during this period.

The Sensitive Period for walking is probably the most readily identified by the adult. Montessori viewed this time as a second birth for the child, for it heralded his passing from a helpless to an active being. One fact Montessori observed during this period is not always recognized by adults: children at this time love to go on very long walks. Montessori found that children as young as a year and a half can walk several miles without tiring. The child does not walk, however, as an adult, who walks steadily with an external goal in mind.

The small child walks to develop his powers, he is building up his being. He goes slowly. He has neither rhythmic step nor goal. But things around him allure him and urge him forward. If the adult would be of help, he must renounce his own rhythm and his own aim. [17]

A fourth Sensitive Period involves an intense interest in objects so tiny and so detailed they may escape our notice entirely. The child may become absorbed by tiny insects barely visible to the human eye. It is as if nature set aside a special period for exploring and appreciating her mysteries, which will later be overlooked by a busy adult.

A fifth Sensitive Period is revealed through an interest in the social aspects of life. The child becomes deeply involved in understanding the civil rights of others and establishing a community with them. He attempts to learn manners and to serve others as well as himself. This social interest is exhibited first as an observing activity, and later develops into a desire for more active contact with others.

Montessori considered her discovery of the Sensitive Periods as one of her most valuable contributions and their further study an important task for educators.

> Before these revelations of true child nature, the laws governing the building up of psychological life had remained absolutely unknown. The study of the Sensitive Periods as directing the formation of man may become one of the sciences of the greatest practical use to mankind.[18]

The Sensitive Periods describe the pattern the child follows in gaining knowledge of his environment. The phenomenon of the Absorbent Mind explains the special quality and process by which he accomplishes this knowledge.

Because the child's mind is not yet formed, he must learn in a different way from the adult. The adult has a knowledge of his environment on which to build, but the child must begin with nothing. It is the Absorbent Mind that accomplishes this seemingly impossible task. It permits an unconscious absorption of the environment by means of a special pre-conscious state of mind. Through this process, the child incorporates knowledge directly into his psychic life. "Impressions do not merely enter his mind, they form it, they incarnate themselves in him." [19] An unconscious activity thus prepares the mind. It is "succeeded by a conscious process which slowly awakens and takes from the unconscious what it can offer." [20] The child constructs his mind in this way until, little by little, he has established memory, the power to understand, and the ability to reason. This creating by absorption extends to all the mental and moral characteristics that are regarded as fixed in humanity or race or community and include patriotism, religion, social habits, technical dispositions, prejudices, and, in fact, all items that make up the sum-total of human personalty.[21]

By the age of three, the unconscious preparation necessary for later development and activity is established. The child now embarks on a new mission, the development of his mental functions. "Before three, the functions are being created; after three, they develop." [22]

Montessori philosophy states, then, that the child contains a "spiritual embryo" or pattern of psychic development even before birth. The two conditions of an integral relationship with the environment and freedom for the child must exist if this embryo is to develop according to its plan. The goal of the child is to so develop, and he is intrinsically motivated toward this goal with an intensity unequalled in all of creation. Since he must create himself out of undeveloped psychic structures, he has been given special internal aids for the task: the Sensitive Periods and the Absorbent Mind. The principles or natural laws governing the child's psychic growth reveal themselves only through the process of his development. By giving the children of the Casa dei Bambini an open environment in which to operate, Montessori was able to observe these natural laws at work in the children and to make a beginning in their identification.

One of the most important of those she observed is the law of work. Montessori had observed that the children in the Casa dei Bambini had achieved an integration of self through their work. They appeared immensely pleased, peaceful, and rested after the most strenuous concentration on tasks they had freely chosen to do. All destructive behavior, whether aggressive and hostile or passive and listless, had disappeared. Montessori concluded that some great need of the child must have been met through this activity of concentration and that the new state of psychic integration the child had thereby reached was actually his normal state.

Montessori referred to this process of psychic integration as the normalization of the child.

> Among the revelations the child has brought us, there is one of fundamental importance, the phenomenon of normalization through work. . . . It is certain that the child's aptitude for work represents a vital instinct; for without work his personality cannot organize itself and deviates from the normal lines of its construction. Man builds himself through working.[23]

It is because work helps the child to become truly himself that he is driven to his constant activity and effort. He follows a law of maximum effort. He cannot stand still; he is impelled to a continuous conquest. "To succeed by himself he intensifies his efforts." [24] Because it fulfills his individual destiny, he appears rested and satisfied after his labors, despite their intensity.

It is obvious that the work of the child is very unlike the work of the adult. Children use the environment to improve themselves; adults use themselves to improve the environment. Children work for the sake of process; adults work to achieve an end result. "It is the adult's task to build an environment superimposed on nature, an outward work calling for activity and intelligent effort; it is what we call productive work, and is by its nature social, collective and organized." [25] He must, therefore, follow a law of exerting minimum effort to attain maximum productivity. He will look both for gain and for assistance. The child seeks no assistance in his work. He must accomplish it by himself.

Because of the social nature of his life, which is neither adaptive nor productive to adult society, the contemporary child is largely removed from it. He is exiled in a school where too often his capacity for constructive growth and self-realization is repressed. This problem in contemporary civilization increases as the adult's role becomes ever more complex.

In primitive societies, where work was simple and could be carried out at a relaxed pace, the adult could coexist with children in his working environment with less friction. The complexity of modern life is making it increasingly difficult for the adult to suspend his own activities "to follow the child, adapting himself to the child's rhythm and the psychological needs of his growth." [26]

A second principle revealed through the child's development is the law of independence. "Except when he has regressive tendencies, the child's nature is to aim directly and energetically at functional independence. Development takes the form of a drive toward an ever greater independence." [27] He uses this independence to listen to his own inner guide for actions that can be useful to him. "Inner forces affect his choice, and if someone usurps the function of this guide, the child is prevented from developing either his will or his concentration." [28] It is because the adult persists in just this usurping that much of the child's potential is never realized. Full personality development is totally dependent on progressive release from external direction and reliance.

A third psychic principle involves the power of attention. At a certain stage in his development, the child begins to direct his attention to particular objects in his environment with an intensity and interest not seen before. "The essential thing is for the task to arouse such an interest that it engages the child's whole personality." [29] This is not the point of arrival, but the point of departure, for the child uses this new ability for concentration to consolidate and develop his personality. At first, he will be attracted to materials that appeal to his instinctive interest, such as bright colors. As he has more experience, however, he builds up an internal knowledge of the "known," which now excites expectation and interest in the novel unknown.

The child concentrates on those things that he already has in his mind, that he has absorbed in the previous period, for whatever has been conquered has a tendency to remain in the mind, to be pondered.[30]

In this way, a discerning interest based on intellect replaces an instinctive interest based on primitive impulses. When the child achieves this focusing of attention based on intellectual interest, he grows calmer and more controlled. His pleasure in his acts of concentration is obvious, and he appears rested and fulfilled. Montessori saw these outward manifestations of pleasure as evidence of the constant element of internal formation taking place in the child.

After internal coordination is established through the child's ability for prolonged attention and concentration, a fourth psychic principle involving the will is revealed. The will's "development is a slow process that evolves through a continuous activity in relationship with the environment." [31] The child chooses a task and must then inhibit his impulses toward extraneous movements. An inner formation of the will is gradually developed through this adaptation to the limits of a chosen task. Decision and action then are the bases for the will's development. Lectures on what the child ought to do are of no use, since they do not involve decision or action. Similarly, it is not moral vision, but this inner formation developed by exercising the will, that gives the strength to control one's actions. Because traditional schooling severely limits the child's opportunities for choice and action, Montessori felt it "not only denies the child every opportunity for using his will but directly obstructs and inhibits its expression." [32]

Montessori observed three stages in the development of the child's will. First, the child begins the repetition of an activity. This repetition occurs after his attention has been polarized and he has achieved a degree of concentration in one of the exercises. The child may repeat the exercise's cycle of activity many times with obvious satisfaction. This "achievement, however trivial to the adult, gives a sense of power and independence to the child." [33] If adults persist in interrupting the child during this cycle of repetition, his self-confidence and ability to persevere in a task are severely jeopardized. Constant interruption during this time is so upsetting to the child that Montessori felt it caused him to live in a state "similar to a permanent nightmare." [34]

After achieving independence and power over his own movements, the child moves to a second stage in the development of the will, where he begins spontaneously to choose self-discipline as a way of life. He makes this choice for his own liberation as a person. It is a point of departure, not an end, which leads him to self-knowledge and self-possession. It is a state characterized by activity, not the immobility that is often referred to as "discipline" in the traditional school. In this stage the child makes creative use of his abilities, accepts the responsibility of his own actions, and complies with the limits of reality.

After achieving self-discipline, the child reaches a third stage of the developed will involving the power to obey. This power is a natural phenomenon, and "shows itself spontaneously and unexpectedly at the end of a long process of maturation." [35]

The phenomenon of obedience is perhaps the most difficult aspect of Montessori philosophy for Americans today to understand or accept. To suggest that children might naturally develop obedience toward their teacher stirs fear that they might become dependent slaves to the adult world and the status quo. This occurs in part because Western thought customarily considers will and obedience as two separate values or powers. This is the result of educational practices of the past, which involved suppressing the child's will in order that it might be substituted with the teacher's will. Unquestioning obedience was thus sought through a process of breaking the child's will. Montessori, on the contrary, considered obedience and will as integral parts of the same phenomenon, obedience occurring as a final stage in the development of the will.

In order to follow this thinking, it is necessary to understand the source of the will in Montessori philosophy. The will is conceived not as an independent force, but as proceeding from a great universal power or "horme." The horme is defined as a vital energy or urge to purposive activity.

> This universal force is not physical, but is the force of life itself in the process of evolution. It drives every form of life irresistibly toward evolution, and from it come the impulses to action. But evolution does not occur by luck, or by chance, but is governed by fixed laws, and if man's life is an expression of that force, his behavior must be molded by it.
>
> In the little child's life, as soon as he makes an action deliberately, of his own accord, this force has begun to enter into his consciousness. What we call his will has begun to develop, and this process continues henceforward, but only as a result of experience. Hence, we are beginning to think of the will not as something inborn, but as something which has to be developed and, because it is a part of nature, this development can only occur in obedience to natural laws. . . . Its development is a slow process that evolves through a continuous activity in relationship with the environment.[36]

When the final stage of this development is reached, obedience to the forces of life appears, and it is this obedience that makes possible the continuance of human life and society.

> Will and obedience then go hand in hand, inasmuch as the will is a prior foundation in the order of development and obedience is a later stage resting on this foundation. . . . Indeed, if the human soul did not possess this quality, if men had never acquired, by some form of evolutionary process, this capacity for obedience, social life would be impossible.[37]

Montessori is not here discussing the blind obedience that has been so much a part of our contemporary culture and which has led to so much horror and destruction.

The most casual glance at what is happening in the world is enough to show us how obedient people are. This kind of obedience is the real reason why vast masses of human beings can be hurled so easily to destruction. It is an uncontrolled form of obedience, an obedience which brings whole nations to ruin. There is no lack of obedience in our world; quite the contrary! . . . What unhappily is absent is the control of obedience.[38]

Control of obedience rests on two conditions: the complete development of obedience through its several stages and the reaching of the final stage in the development of the will. Obedience develops in stages, much as other characteristics of human beings.

At first it is dictated purely by the hormic impulse, then it rises to the level of consciousness, and thereafter it goes on developing, stage by stage, till it comes under the control of the conscious will.[39]

This conscious will, if it has developed under natural circumstances, cannot lead to destructive acts because it has as its source the forces of life:

But the real facts of the situation are that the will does not lead to disorder and violence. These are signs of emotional disturbance and suffering. Under proper conditions, the will is a force which impels activities beneficial to life. Nature imposes on the child the task of growing up, and his will leads him to make progress and to develop his powers.[40]

When Montessori philosophy then speaks of obedience, it is referring to a natural characteristic of the human being. This natural characteristic must be developed into a controlled or intelligent obedience, a cooperation with the forces of life and nature on which the survival of human life and society depends.

George Dennison is a contemporary writer who has a good feel for this growth of intelligent obedience and cooperation in the child, and the way in which they become established in ongoing relationships between adult and child. In Dennison's view, the child comes to recognize the "natural authority of adults" through his experience first with his parents and later with other adults in his world. They accept him, but in their caring for him they also place certain demands on him. In his superb book *The Lives of Children,* Dennison describes this relationship developing with a boy named José.

> My own demands then were an important part of José's experience. They were not simply the demands of a teacher, nor of an adult, but belonged to my own way of caring about José. And he sensed this. There was something he prized in the fact that I made demands on him. . . . We became collaborators in the business of life. . . . What he prized, after all, was this: that an adult, with a life of his own, was willing to teach him. . . . To the extent that he sensed my life stretching out beyond him into (for him) the unknown, my meaning as an adult was enhanced, and the things I already knew and might teach him gained the luster they really possess in life.[41]

A fifth psychic principle—the development of the intelligence—governs the key to understanding life itself. This is the "key which sets in motion the mechanisms essential to education." [42] Intelligence is defined as "the sum of those reflex and associative or reproductive activities which enable the mind to construct itself, putting it into relation with the environment." [43]

The beginning of intellectual development is the consciousness of difference or distinction in the environment. The child makes these perceptions through his senses; he must then organize them into an orderly arrangement in his mind. It will do him no good to have had contact with a stimulating and varied environment if it only results in a chaos of mental impressions. "To help the development of the intelligence is to help to put the images of the consciousness in order." [44] The first sign that this internal process is taking place will be quickness of response to stimuli, and the second will be the orderliness of these responses.

A sixth natural law governs the development of the child's imagination and creativity. These are inborn powers in the child that develop as his mental capacities are established through his interaction with the environment. The environment must itself be beautiful, harmonious, and based on reality in order for the child to organize his perceptions of it. When he has developed realistic and ordered perceptions of the life about him, the child is capable of the selecting and emphasizing processes necessary for creative endeavors. He "abstracts the dominant characteristics of things, and thus succeeds in associating their images, and keeping them in the foreground of consciousness." [45] Montessori emphasized that this selective capability requires three qualities: a remarkable power of attention and concentration which appear almost as a form of meditation; a considerable autonomy and independence of judgment; and an expectant faith that remains open to truth and reality.

Montessori was particularly concerned with the latter quality, for she felt adults often inadvertently hinder its development in children. The young child has a tendency to create fantasies and dwell on them. Adults have been accustomed to consider these as proof of the child's superior imaginative abilities. Montessori considered them proof not of his imagination, but of his dependent and powerless position in life. "An adult resigns himself to his lot; a child creates an illusion." [46] Similarly, Montessori regarded the child's belief in the fruit of the adult's imaginations—such as the Santa Claus tradition—as proof not of the child's imagination, but of his credulity, a credulity that disappears as he matures and his intelligence develops. The adult substitutes his imagination for the child's because he continually sees the child as a passive being for whom he must act.

> The child is usually considered as a receptive being instead of as an active being, and this happens in every department of his life. Even imagination is so treated; fairy tales and stories of enchanted princesses are told with a view to encouraging the child's imagination. But when he listens to these and other

kinds of story, he is only receiving impressions. He is not developing his own powers to imagine constructively.[47]

In addition to an environment of beauty, order, and reality, Montessori realized that the child needs freedom if he is to develop creativity—freedom to select what attracts him in his environment, to relate to it without interruption and for as long as he likes, to discover solutions and ideas and select his answer on his own, and to communicate and share his discoveries with others at will. The child's alienation or detachment, characteristic of most of these phases of the creative process, has been widely recognized by visitors to Montessori classrooms. However, its source is not always properly identified. Often observers are merely sensitive to a child's temporary isolation from his fellows, and do not recognize this state as a part of the creative process itself.

The child in the Montessori classroom is also free from the judgment by an outside authority that so annihilates the creative impulse. This is in direct contrast to the traditional school setting, where the basis for evaluation is always outside the child. The disastrous results of this controlling and constantly judging classroom environment are sensitively recorded in John Holt's book *How Children Fail*. In contrast to traditional education, Montessori deserves credit for an early appreciation of the scope of creativity and for developing better means for encouraging it than had hitherto been devised.[48]

A seventh psychic principle deals with the development of the emotional and spiritual life of the child. Montessori believed the child possesses within him at birth the senses that respond to his emotional and spiritual environment and thereby develop his capacity for loving and understanding responses to others and to God. These inborn senses correspond to those possessed at birth for responding to the physical world and thereby developing the intelligence. The child achieves the development of the latter through the stimuli of the material world, but for the former he needs the stimuli of human beings. He is first aroused through a loving experience with his mother. Her love for him awakens his internal senses and makes possible, in turn, his loving responses to her. Once the child's emotional awakening has thus occurred, he will begin to respond to the offer of loving relationships from others. It is the wealth of emotional material in others that will attract him, even as the richness of physical stimuli attract him to his material environment. The attraction is delicate and subtle, and can be destroyed as easily in dealing with the emotional life as with the intellectual life. Therefore, the free choice of the child must again be respected. If the adult has been careful to present the child with the means he needs for his development and to be always ready to help, but never to dominate, then the child will assuredly respond to the adult's love and respect. "The day will come when his spirit will become sensitive to our spirit. . . . The power to obey us, to communicate his conquests to us, to share his joys with us, will be the new element in his life." [49] Finally, he will begin responding to other children as well, showing an awareness and interest in their work and progress as well as his own.

To achieve emotional and spiritual maturity, the child must develop not only his internal capacity for love, but also his moral sense. Again, Montessori believed this to be an internal sense present at birth. "It is not surprising that there should be an internal sensation which warns us of perils, and causes us to recognize the circumstances favorable to life." [50] For the development of the moral sense to take place, the child needs an environment in which good and evil are clearly differentiated. This "good and evil" is not to be confused with acquired social habits, but is of an ultimate nature, and bound up with life itself. "Good is life; evil is death; the real distinction is as clear as the words." [51]

An eighth psychic principle is related to the stages of a child's growth. Montessori observed that the child's development occurs in stages that can be fairly well defined by chronological age. She outlined five such periods of growth. The period from birth to three years is characterized by unconscious growth and absorption. The internal structure of emotional and intellectual development is being created by means of the Sensitive Periods and Absorbent Mind. This is a period of unequalled energy and intense effort for the child, for indeed his whole life will depend upon what he can accomplish. During the period between three and six, the child gradually brings the knowledge of his unconscious to a conscious level. By six, his inner formation of discipline and obedience has been established, and he has developed an internal model of reality on which to base his imaginative and creative efforts. Between six and nine, then, he is capable of building the academic and artistic skills essential for a life of fulfillment in his culture. In the period from nine to twelve, the child is ready to open himself to knowledge of the universe itself. It is similar to the earlier period from birth to three, when he eagerly absorbed everything in his environment. However, he is now learning with his conscious mind, and, instead of being limited to his immediate environment, he can range as far as the cosmos itself. His intellectual interest for a lifetime will depend upon his opportunities during this period. This is why his schooling at this time must include as complete an exposure to the world as possible, and not be broken down into isolated units of subject matter as is now customary in traditional schools. The period from twelve to eighteen is the time for exploring more concentrated areas of interest in depth. The child should be choosing the pattern of endeavor he will follow for life, and so it is a period of limiting choices. This period of decision is postponed in our culture until a later age. Since it is usually not encouraged or even permitted at the natural age, unnecessary emotional and intellectual problems occur. The adolescent rebellion so taken for granted in our culture is a phenomenon not seen in many other civilizations. Montessori's background in anthropology may have been a principal reason for her insight into these problems of adolescence based on cultural patterns.

Because it was through observation of the child that Montessori made her discoveries of the Sensitive Periods, the Absorbent Mind, and the natural laws governing psychic development, she determined that education must have a new goal: to study and observe the child himself from the moment of his conception. Only in this way can a new education based on aiding the inner powers of the child be developed to replace the present method, which is based on the transmission of past knowledge. If this could be done, Montessori felt, there would be hope for our troubled world.

Alone a scientific enquiry into human personality can lead us to salvation, and we have before us in the child a psychic entity, a social group of immense size, a veritable world-power if rightly used. If salvation and help are to come, it is from the child, for the child is the construction of man, and so of society. The child is endowed with an inner power which can guide us to a more luminous future. Education should no longer be mostly imparting of knowledge, but must take a new path, seeking the release of human potentialities. When should such education begin? Our answer is that the greatness of human personality begins at birth, an affirmation full of practical reality, however strikingly mystic.

Scientific observation then has established that education is not what the teacher gives; education is a natural process spontaneously carried out by the human individual, and is acquired not by listening to words but by experiences upon the environment. The task of the teacher becomes that of preparing a series of motives of cultural activity, spread over a specially prepared environment, and then refraining from obtrusive interference. Human teachers can only help the great work that is being done, as servants help the master. Doing so, they will be witnesses to the unfolding of the human soul and to the rising of a New Man who will not be the victim of events, but will have the clarity of vision to direct and shape the future of human society.[52]

3

The Montessori Method

UNLIKE MANY educational philosophers, Montessori developed an educational method to implement her philosophy. Her genius in this respect is an important reason for the enduring and widespread impact of her work. It should be kept in mind, however, that Montessori wanted her method to be considered an open-minded one, and not a fixed system. She believed in innovation in the classroom, and her whole approach to education was in the spirit of constant experimentation based on observation of the child.

There are two key components to the Montessori method: the environment, including the educational materials and exercises; and the teachers who prepare this environment. Montessori considered her emphasis on the environment a primary element in her method. She described this environment as a nourishing place for the child. It is designed to meet his needs for self-construction and to reveal his personality and growth patterns to us. This means that not only must it contain what the child needs in a positive sense, but all obstacles to his growth must be removed from it as well.

Although Montessori placed this unusual emphasis on the environment, it is important to keep three ideas in mind. First, she regarded the environment as secondary to life itself. "It can modify in that it can help or hinder, but it can never create. . . . The origins of the development both in the species and in the individual, lie within." [1] The child then does not grow because he happens to be placed in a nourishing environment. "He grows because the potential life within him develops, making itself visible." [2] Second, the environment must be carefully prepared for the child by a knowledgeable and sensitive adult. Third, the adult must be a participant in the child's living and growing within it.

> Plainly, the environment must be a living one, directed by a higher intelligence, arranged by an adult who is prepared for his mission. It is in this that our conception differs both from that of the world in which the adult does everything for the child and from that of a passive environment in which the adult abandons the child to himself . . . This means that it is not enough to set the child among objects in proportion to his size and strength; the adult who is to help him must have learned how to do so.[3]

If the teacher is to play this key role in the environment for the child, she clearly must be open to life and the process of becoming herself. If she is a rigid person for whom life has become existing rather than growing, she will not be able to prepare a living environment for the children. Her classroom will be a static place, rather than one actively responsive to the continually changing needs of a growing child. It is essential to keep this understanding in mind before going on to a description of the Montessori environment; much will depend on the teacher's ability to participate with the children in a life of becoming.

There are six basic components to the Montessori classroom environment. They deal with the concepts of freedom, structure and order, reality and nature, beauty and atmosphere, the Montessori materials, and the development of community life.

Freedom is an essential element in a Montessori environment for two reasons. First, it is only in an atmosphere of freedom that the child can reveal himself to us. Since the duty of the educator is to identify and aid the child's psychic development, he must have an opportunity to observe the child in as free and open an environment as possible. If a new education is "to arise from the study of the individual, such study must occupy itself with the observation of free children." [4] Second, if the child possesses within himself the pattern for his own development, this inner guide must be allowed to direct the child's growth.

Although previous educators had espoused liberty for the child, Montessori had a new concept in mind.

> It is true that some pedagogues, led by Rousseau, have given voice to impractical principles and vague aspirations for the liberty of the child, but the true concept of liberty is practically unknown to educators.[5]

The freedom referred to by earlier educators was often a negative reaction to earlier domination—a release from oppressive bonds or previous submission to authority which results in an outpouring of disorder and primitive impulses. Montessori regarded a child given freedom in this situation as at the mercy of his deviations, and not in command of his own will. He would not be free at all.

Montessori believed that freedom for the child depended upon a previous development and construction of his personality involving his independence, will, and inner discipline. "Real freedom . . . is a consequence of development . . . of latent guides, aided by education." [6] These latent guides within the child direct him toward the independence, will, and discipline essential for his freedom. How is he to be aided in their development? First, he must be helped toward independence through his environment. "The absurd mistake in envisaging the freedom of the child in education has lain in imagining his hypothetical independence of the adult without corresponding preparation of the environment." [7] The child must be given activities that encourage independence, and he must not be served by others in acts he can learn to perform for himself.

No one can be free unless he is independent: therefore, the first, active manifestations of the child's individual liberty must be so guided that through this activity he may arrive at independence. . . .

We habitually serve children; and this is not only an act of servility toward them, but it is dangerous, since it tends to suffocate their useful, spontaneous activity. . . .

Our duty toward him is, in every case, that of helping him to make a conquest of such useful acts as nature intended he should perform.[8]

Second, the child must be aided in developing his will by being encouraged to coordinate his actions toward a given end and to achieve something he himself has chosen to do. Adults must be on their guard against tyrannizing him and substituting their wills for his.

Third, the child must be aided in developing discipline by being provided with opportunities for constructive work. "To obtain discipline . . . it is not necessary for the adult to be a guide or mentor in conduct, but to give the child the opportunities of work." [9] The process whereby inner discipline results from the child's work will be discussed in more detail later, but its key role should be kept in mind.

Fourth, the child must be aided in developing a clear understanding of good and evil. "The first idea that the child must acquire, in order to be actively disciplined, is that of the difference between good and evil." [10] To achieve this distinction, the adult must set firm limits against destructive and asocial actions.

The liberty of the child should have as its limit the collective interest; as its form, what we universally consider good breeding. We must, therefore, check in the child whatever offends or annoys others, or whatever tends toward rough or ill-bred acts.[11]

Montessori described a classroom that had achieved her concept of free operation as "a room in which all the children move about usefully, intelligently, and voluntarily, without committing any rough or rude act." [12]

In striving to develop this freedom, it should be clearly established that only the destructive acts of the child are to be limited. "All the rest—every manifestation having a useful scope—whatever it be, and under whatever form it expresses itself, must not only be permitted but must be observed by the teacher." [13]

The children are, therefore, free to move about the classroom at will—ideally to an outside environment, weather permitting, as well as inside the classroom. Montessori described this outside environment as an "open-air space, which is to be in direct communication with the schoolroom, so that the children may be free to go and come as they like, throughout the entire day." [14] Because of this freedom of movement, a Montessori day is not divided between work periods and rest or play periods, as is accepted practice in traditional schools.

The children are free to choose their own activities in the classroom, again keeping in mind "that here we do not speak of useless or dangerous acts, for these must be suppressed." [15] This protection of the child's choice is a key element in the Montessori method, and it must not be violated. "It is necessary rigorously to avoid the arrest of spontaneous movements and the imposition of arbitrary tasks." [16] In order to have a choice of activities, the child must be presented with a variety of exercises designed for his auto-education.

> The child, left at liberty to exercise his activities, ought to find in his surroundings something organized in direct relation to his internal organization which is developing itself by natural laws.[17]

A true choice will depend upon a knowledge of the exercises. Before using the materials, then, the child must have an introduction to them either through an individual lesson given by the teacher or by observing their use by another child.

Because they momentarily impose on the child's freedom, these lessons are brief.

> We admit every lesson infringes the liberty of the child, and for this reason we allow it to last only for a few seconds. . . . It is in the subsequent free choice, and the repetition of the exercise, as in the subsequent activity, spontaneous, associative, and reproductive, that the child will be left "free." [18]

In order not to interfere with the child's free choice of activity, there are no artificially induced competitions or rewards and punishments in the Montessori classroom.

> Such prizes and punishments are . . . the instrument of slavery for the spirit. . . . The prize and the punishment are incentives toward unnatural or forced effort, and therefore we certainly cannot speak of the natural development of the child in connection with them.[19]

The children are given as much freedom to work out their own social relations with each other as possible. Montessori felt that, for the most part, children like to solve their social problems, and that adults cause harm by too early and frequent interference.

> When adults interfere in this first stage of preparation for social life, they nearly always make mistakes. . . . Problems abound at every step and it gives the children great pleasure to face them. They feel irritated if we intervene, and find a way if left to themselves.[20]

Unlike traditional classrooms, the children speak to each other and initiate activities together whenever they like. They are not forced, subtly or otherwise, to join in any group activities or to share themselves with others when they are not ready or interested. Because they are not forced to compete with each other, their natural desire to help others develops spontaneously. This phenomenon is particularly interesting to watch in the older and younger children in the classroom, whose age differential may be as much as four years.

Because the Montessori approach to the social life of the children is different from that of a traditional classroom, the emphasis on it is often missed.

> Teachers who use direct methods cannot understand how social behavior is fostered in a Montessori school. They think it offers scholastic material but not social material. They say, "If the child does everything on his own, what becomes of social life?" But what is social life if not the solving of social problems, behaving properly, and pursuing aims acceptable to all? To them, social life consists in sitting side by side and hearing someone else talk; but that is just the opposite. The only social life that children get in the ordinary schools is during playtime or on excursions. Ours live always in an active community.[21]

Through the freedom he is given in a Montessori environment, the child has a unique opportunity to reflect upon his own actions, to determine their consequences both for himself and for others, to test himself against the limits of reality, to learn what gives him a sense of fulfillment and what leaves him feeling empty and dissatisfied, and to discover both his capabilities and his shortcomings. The opportunity to develop self-knowledge is one of the most important results of freedom in a Montessori classroom.

A second key element in the Montessori environment is its structure and order. The underlying structure and order of the universe must be reflected in the classroom if the child is to internalize it, and thus build his own mental order and intelligence. Through this internalized order, the child learns to trust his environment and his power to interact with it in a positive way. It insures for the child the possibility of purposeful activity. He knows where to go to find the materials of his choice. To assist him in his choice, the materials are grouped according to the interest they appeal to, and arranged in sequence as to their difficulty or the degree of complication.

Order means that the child is assured the possibility of a completed cycle of activity in using the materials. He will find all the pieces needed for the exercise he chooses; nothing will be broken or missing. No one will be permitted to interrupt him or to interfere with his work. He will return the materials to the place—and in the condition—in which he found them. By returning the materials, the child not only participates in the full cycle of activity, but becomes an integral partner in maintaining the order of the classroom. The matter-of-fact way in which the child accepts this responsibility in a Montessori classroom often comes as a surprise to parent and educator alike. We are accustomed to observing children in environments that are not structured for their needs, and therefore we do not often have an opportunity to witness this aspect of their developing natures.

Although it is essential that the environment be ordered, it is not necessary or desirable for every item to remain in exactly the same place. In practice, an alert teacher will find it necessary to rearrange continuously many individual items in the environment in order to keep it a living place, responsive to the children as they grow. For example, a teacher who feels a piece of material may have become part of the background and thus overlooked, or who wishes to draw a child's attention to an exercise without obvious direction, may place the material on a table in a prominent part of the room for a day or two. The teacher will find the flexibility she needs to maintain the necessary order in the classroom, without creating a static environment, if she keeps in mind the underlying purpose of structure for the child: it is not to serve the needs of insecure or rigid adults, but to aid children in building their intelligence and trust in the environment.

A third component of the Montessori environment is its emphasis on reality and nature. The child must have the opportunity to internalize the limits of nature and reality if he is to be freed from his fantasies and illusions, both physical and psychological. Only in this way can he develop the self-discipline and security he needs to explore his external and internal worlds and to become an acute and appreciative observer of life. The equipment in the classroom, therefore, is geared to bringing the child into closer contact with reality. A refrigerator, stove, sink, and telephone are all authentic. The silver to be polished is tarnished. Nourishing food is prepared and served. Not only is the equipment realistic, but it is not designed to hide and therefore encourage errors. The furniture is light, and reasonable care must be taken not to knock it over. Often real glasses are used for juice, a heated iron for ironing, a sharp knife for cutting vegetables.

Also in keeping with the real world, where everyone cannot have the same thing at once, there is only one piece of each type of equipment in the Montessori classroom. Because he has no alternative, the child learns to wait until another is finished if the exercise he wants is in use. "The child comes to see that he must respect the work of others, not because someone has said he must, but because this is a reality he meets in his daily experience." [22]

Montessori emphasized the importance of contact with nature for the developing child. Man "still belongs to nature, and, especially when he is a child, he must needs draw from it the forces necessary to the development of the body and of the spirit." [23] The method she favored for the initial contact with nature was through the care of plants and animals.[24] Montessori was aware that, with the spread of urban life, it would be increasingly difficult to satisfy this deep need of the child. She was, however, insistent:

There must, however, be provision for the child to have contact with Nature; to understand and appreciate the order, the harmony, and the beauty in Nature; and also to master the natural laws which are the basis of all sciences and arts, so that the child may better understand and participate in the marvelous things which civilization creates. Speeding up the march of civilization and at the same time being in touch with Nature create a difficult social problem. It thus becomes a duty of society to satisfy the needs of the child at various stages of development, if the child and consequently society and mankind are not to go under but are to advance on the road of progress.[25]

This emphasis on nature should permeate the atmosphere of the Montessori environment, and be one of its most readily recognizable components. The room and outside area should be alive with growing things of all kinds which are cared for by the children. In addition, there should be magnifying glasses, microscopes, and simple experiments of many varieties for the children to perform themselves. Perhaps most important of all, the children must have unhurried time in the woods and country to discover oneness with creation and absorb the wonder of the natural world.

Closely connected with an emphasis on nature is a fourth concept fundamental to the Montessori environment—beauty and an atmosphere that encourages a positive and spontaneous response to life. Perhaps because Dr. Montessori began her life as an educator with children from insane asylums and slums, she was particularly sensitive to this need of the child. She regarded beauty not as an extra aid for the developing child, but as a positive need in calling forth his power to respond to life. Because true beauty is based upon simplicity, the classroom need not be an elaborate place; but everything within it must be of good design and quality, and as carefully and attractively displayed as a well-planned exhibit. The colors should be bright and cheerful, and harmoniously arranged. The atmosphere of the room must be relaxing and warm, and invite participation.

A fifth component of the classroom, the Montessori equipment, is widely publicized and its role often misunderstood. Because of their visibility, the Montessori materials tend to be overemphasized in relation to the other elements in the Montessori method. In addition, their purpose is often confused. They are not learning equipment in the conventional sense, because their aim is not the external one of teaching children skills or imparting knowledge through "correct usage." [26] Rather, the aim is an internal one of assisting the child's self-construction and psychic development. They aid this growth by providing the child with stimuli that capture his attention and initiate a process of concentration.

> The first essential for the child's development is concentration. . . . He must find out how to concentrate, and for this he needs things to concentrate upon. . . . Indeed, it is just here that the importance of our schools really lies. They are places in which the child can find the kind of work that permits him to do this.[27]

If the teacher has materials to offer that polarize the child's attention, he will find it possible to give the child the freedom he needs for his development.[28]

In order to serve their purpose of internal formation, the materials must correspond to the child's inner needs. This means that any individual material must be presented to the child at the right moment in his development. Montessori suggested age levels for introducing each of her materials to the child; however, the sensitive moment for introduction to any individual child must be determined by observation and experimentation. The teacher watches for the quality of concentration in the child and for a spontaneous repetition of his actions with a material. These responses will indicate the meaningfulness of the material to him at that particular moment in his growth and whether the intensity of the stimulus which that material represents for him is also matched to his internal needs. Both the material itself and the intensity of stimulus it presents can be varied to meet the child's inner needs.[29] The quantity of the stimuli also must be adjusted to the child's needs.

> An excessive quantity of the educative material . . . may dissipate the attention, render the exercises with the objects me-

chanical, and cause the child to pass by his psychological moment of ascent without perceiving it and seizing it. . . . Over-abundance debilitates and retard progress; this has been proved again and again.[30]

Because matching the materials to the child's inner needs is essential, there can be no rote following of the designed progression in introducing the materials. The teacher must be flexible in altering the sequence or omitting materials an individual child shows no need for.

Because educational materials of the past had been designed for a passive child waiting to receive instructions, Montessori considered her materials a "scientific departure" from the past. Her materials instead are based on

the conception of an active personality—reflex and associative—developing itself by a series of reactions induced by systematic stimuli which have been determined by experiment. This new pedagogy accordingly belongs to the series of modern sciences. . . . The "method" which informs it—namely, experiment, observation, evidence or proof, the recognition of new phenomena, their reproduction and utilization—undoubtedly place it among the experimental sciences.[31]

This new approach to education, suggested to her by the work of Itard and Séguin, was regarded by Montessori as her "initial contribution to education" and "the key" to the continuation of her work.[32]

In addition to meaningfulness to the child, there are at least five other principles involved in the determining of Montessori materials. First, the difficulty or the error that the child is to discover and understand must be isolated in a single piece of material. This isolation simplifies the child's task for him and enables him to perceive the problem more readily. A tower of blocks will present to the child only a variation in size from block to block—not a variation in size, color, designs, and noises, such as are often found in block towers in American toy stores.

Second, the materials progress from simple to more complex design and usage. A first set of numerical rods to teach seriation vary in length only. After discovering length sensorially through these rods, a second set, colored red and blue, in one-meter dimension, can be used to associate numbers and length and to understand simple problems of addition and subtraction. A third set of rods, much smaller in size because the initial dependence on sensorial learning and motor development has been passed, is used in association with a board chart for more complicated mathematical problems and the introduction of writing numerical problems.

Third, the materials are designed to prepare the child indirectly for future learning. The development of writing is a good example of this indirect preparation. From the beginning, knobs on materials, by which the child lifts and manipulates them, have acted to coordinate his finger and thumb motor action. Through the making of designs that involves using metal insets to guide his movements, the child has developed the ability to use a pencil. By tracing sandpaper letters with his finger, he has developed a muscle memory of the pattern for forming letters. When the day arrives that the child is motivated to write, he can do so with a minimum of frustration and anxiety. This principle of indirect preparation enables the child to experience success in his endeavors much more readily and aids the development of self-confidence and initiative.

Fourth, the materials begin as concrete expressions of an idea and gradually become more and more abstract representations. A solid wooden triangle is sensorially explored. Separate pieces of wood representing its base and sides are then presented, and the triangle's dimensions discovered. Later, flat wooden triangles are fitted into wooden puzzle trays, then on solidly colored paper triangles, then on triangles outlined with a heavy colored line, and finally on the abstraction of thinly outlined triangles. At a certain stage in this progression, the child will have grasped the abstract essence of the concrete material, and will no longer be dependent upon or show the same interest in them.

> When the instruments [materials] have been constructed with great precision, they provoke a spontaneous exercise so coordinated and so harmonious with the facts of internal development, that at a certain point a new psychical picture, a species of higher plane in the complex development, is revealed. The child turns away spontaneously from the material, not with any signs of fatigue, but rather as if impelled by fresh energies, and his mind is capable of abstractions.[33]

The greater a child's absorption with a piece of material, the more likely that he is making the transition from concrete knowledge to abstract knowledge. This is a natural process that should not be interfered with. If, at this point, the teacher tries to emphasize concrete objects with the child, she will interrupt his natural development.[34]

Montessori materials are designed for auto-education, and the control of error lies in the materials themselves rather than in the teacher. The control of error guides the child in his use of the materials and permits him to recognize his own mistakes.

> "Control of error" is any kind of indicator which tells us whether we are going toward our goal, or away from it. . . . We must provide this as well as instruction and materials on which to work. The power to make progress comes in large measure from having freedom and an assured path along which to go; but to this must also be added some way of knowing if, and when, we have left the path.[35]

This dialogue with the materials puts the child in control of the learning process. The teacher is not to usurp this role by pointing out the child's error to him. If the child cannot see his error in spite of the material's design, it means he has not sufficiently developed to do so. In time, he will be able to see it and will correct his own errors.

A block of wood, in which the child places cylinders of varying sizes in corresponding holes, is an example of control of error designed within the materials. If the cylinders are not matched in the correct holes, there will be one cylinder left over. Again, it is not the problem alone that interests the child and aids his progress:

> What interests the child is the sensation, not only of placing the objects, but of acquiring a new power of perception, enabling him to recognize the difference of dimension in the cylinders.[36]

It is not necessary to design the control of error into all the materials in such a mechanical way as the cylinder block. As the materials progress in complication, the control of error is shifted to the child himself, who has gradually developed his ability to recognize differences of dimension by sight. Control of error is also introduced at a later stage by providing the child with models with which to compare his work. He can find the answers to a certain set of mathematical problems, for example, on a chart board designed for that purpose and freely available to him.

> But, however slight the control of error may be, and in spite of the fact that this diverges more and more from an external mechanism, to rely upon the internal activities which are gradually developing, it always depends, like all the qualities of the objects, upon the fundamental reaction of the child, who accords it prolonged attention, and repeats the exercises.[37]

There are several basic rules in the use of the Montessori materials. Because they are designed for a serious purpose— the child's own development—the children are required to treat them with respect. They are handled carefully, and only after their use is understood. When the child uses an exercise, he brings all the materials necessary and arranges them carefully on a mat or rug in an organized manner. When he is finished, he returns them to the shelf, leaving them in good order for the next child.

The child has a right not to be interrupted when using the materials, either by other children or the teacher. Here the teacher must be very alert. Praise or even a smile from her can distract the child, and children have been known to stop and put their work away with no more interference than this.

The introduction of new material to the child is called the Fundamental Lesson. The purpose of this lesson is not only to present the child with a key to the materials and their possibilities for him, but to enable the teacher to discover more about the child and his inner development. She uses the lesson to observe his reactions, and will experiment with different approaches to him. In this sense, "the lesson corresponds to an experiment." [38] Choosing the right moment to introduce a lesson to the child requires sensitivity and experience. The teacher is momentarily taking the initiative from the child in directing his growth.

> In such a delicate task, a great art must suggest the moment, and limit the intervention, in order that we shall arouse no perturbation, cause no deviation, but rather that we shall help the soul which is coming into the fullness of life, and which shall live from its own forces.[39]

Such lessons will be given almost exclusively on an individual basis. Since no two children can be exactly in the same state of development at one time, the best moment for a specific lesson will not correspond in two cases at once. Further,

> the children being free are not obligated to remain in their places quiet and ready to listen to the teacher, or to watch what she is doing [collective lessons are unlikely to be successful, and cannot be used as a primary source of introducing materials]. The collective lessons, in fact, are of very secondary importance, and have been almost abolished by us.[40]

The Fundamental Lesson is defined as

> a determinate impression of contact with the external world;
> it is the clear, scientific, pre-determined character of this
> contact which distinguishes it from the mass of indetermi-
> nate contacts which the child is continually receiving from his
> surroundings.[41]

In order for this contact to be of definite and clear character,
the teacher must have a thorough knowledge of the materials,
and have determined beforehand by conscientious practice
the exact way in which she is going to present the exercise.
The child responds to the precision of this presentation because it fulfills an inner need for him.

> The child not only needs something interesting to do, but also
> likes to be shown exactly how to do it. Precision is found to
> attract him deeply, and this it is that keeps him at work. From
> this we must infer that his attraction toward these manipula-
> tive tasks has an unconscious aim. The child has an instinct
> to coordinate his movements and to bring them under control.[42]

In addition to precision and orderly presentation, the characteristics of the Fundamental Lesson are brevity, simplicity,
and objectivity. By using few and simple words, the teacher
can more readily convey the truth that lies hidden in the
materials.[43]

> The lesson must be presented in such a way that the personality
> of the teacher shall disappear. There shall remain in evidence
> only the object to which she wishes to call the attention of the
> child.[44]

After the teacher has presented the material in this way,
she invites the child to use the material as she has done.
During this first use of the material by the child, the teacher
remains with him to observe his actions, taking care not to
interfere with his liberty.

The teacher shall observe whether the child interests himself in the object, how he is interested in it, for how long, etc., even noticing the expression of his face. And she must take great care not to offend the principles of liberty. For, if she provokes the child to make an unnatural effort, she will no longer know what is the spontaneous activity of the child. If, therefore, the lesson rigorously prepared in this brevity, simplicity, and truth is not understood by the child, is not accepted by him as an explanation of the object, the teacher must be warned of two things: first, not to insist by repeating the lesson; and second, not to make the child feel that he has made a mistake, or that he is not understood, because in doing so she will cause him to make an effort to understand, and will thus alter the natural state which must be used by her in making her psychological observation.[45]

If the child shows by his responses that the teacher has misjudged her moment of introduction, the teacher suggests they put the material away and use it again another day. If the child shows he was ready for the presentation, the teacher can reinforce the experience subtly through a smile or simple "that's fine," and leave the child to use the material as long as he likes.

Knowing how to use the material is only the beginning of its usefulness to the child. It is in the repetition of its use that real growth for the child—the development of his psychic nature—takes place. This repetition occurs only if the child has understood the idea the exercise represents, and if this idea corresponds to an inner need of the child.

A mental grasp of the idea [of the material] is indispensable to the beginning of repetition. The exercise which develops life, consists in the repetition, not in the mere grasp of the idea . . . This phenomenon does not always occur. . . . In fact, repetition corresponds to a need. . . . It is necessary to offer those exercises which correspond to the need of development felt by an organism.[46]

It is, then, repetition of an exercise that the teacher will watch for. When this phenomenon occurs, she knows she has helped to match the child's inner needs with his environmental aids for development, and she can leave him to direct his own learning.

After a period of repetitive use of an exercise in its originally understood form, yet another phenomenon appears: the child will begin to create new ways in which to use the material, often combining several different exercises that are interrelated or comparing the material to related objects in his environment. It is the child's inner development, combined with the creative possibilities hidden within the design of the materials, that makes this burst of creative activity possible. Because the child doesn't know that many of his own discoveries with the materials have been made by others before, they belong to him in a very special way and enable him to experience the thrill of discovering the unknown for himself.

Because originally the children are shown a way of using the materials so that they can develop some knowledge and skill with them, many people do not realize their potential for developing creativity within the child. They envision children going through rigid and mechanical actions with the material—continuous repetitions of what they have been shown and never leading to new activity. John Dewey viewed the Montessori method in this way, claiming that Montessori had accomplished physical freedom in the classroom but not intellectual freedom:

> But there is no freedom allowed the child to create. He is free to choose which apparatus he will use, but never to choose his own ends, never to bend a material to his own plans. For the material is limited to a fixed number of things which must be handled in a certain way.[47]

One reason educators and parents adopt this limited view of the Montessori materials is that they are not accustomed to seeing very young children work freely with truly creative materials. Most of the toys and materials given to the child are so narrow in scope, design, and purpose that he literally can go nowhere with them. He has to attempt to make them into something else because what is there is totally unsatisfying. He needs no introduction to such materials because there is basically nothing to introduce, nothing waiting there to be discovered. In his search for something of value in them, the child takes them apart, and, because of their flimsy construction, he inadvertently destroys them. The Montessori materials, on the contrary, are carefully designed and constructed with definite purposes in mind. Their continued impact on and interest for children over a period of fifty years is sufficient testimony to their creative possibilities.

Of course, it is possible for the teacher to pre-empt the child's right to make his own discoveries with the Montessori materials, by showing him more than their basic idea, and thus rob him of the joy of creativity that should have been his. Classrooms where this consistently occurs are easily spotted through their mechanical atmosphere. The motions of life can be seen, but not living itself. One Montessori teacher describes such classrooms as "horizontal." It is misuse of the materials on the part of some teachers that accounts for this occurrence, not the method or materials themselves, which are specifically designed to encourage creativity.

After the teacher is convinced that a concept has been established in the child's mind through his use of the materials, she introduces the exact nomenclature to correspond to the new concept. She does this by a method developed by Séguin entitled the "Three Period Lesson." In the first step, the teacher simply associates the name of an object with the abstract idea the name represents, such as the concepts of rough and smooth. She is careful not to confuse the child by introducing any extraneous words or explanations.[48] In the second step, the teacher tests to see if the name is still associated in the child's mind with the object. She asks the child, "which is the red one, which the blue?" or "which is long, which is short?" If the child does not succeed in the association, the teacher does not correct him.

> Indeed, why correct him? If the child has not succeeded in associating the name with the object, the only way in which to succeed would be to repeat both the action of the sense stimuli and the name; in other words, to repeat the lesson. But when the child has failed, we should know that he was not at that instant ready for the psychic association which we wished to provoke in him, and we must therefore choose another moment.[49]

If the child has succeeded in establishing the association desired, the teacher proceeds to the third step, asking the child to pronounce the appropriate vocabulary himself.

After vocabulary is thus established, the child is capable of communicating a generalization of ideas. He finds in his environment objects that correspond to his new knowledge: "the sky is blue" or "the flower smells sweet."

> In dealing with normal children, we must await this spontaneous investigation of the surroundings. . . . In such cases, the children experience a joy at each fresh discovery. They are conscious of a sense of dignity and satisfaction which encourages them to seek for new sensations from their environment and to make themselves spontaneous observers.[50]

The Montessori materials are roughly divided into four categories: the daily-living exercises involving the physical care of person and environment, the sensorial, the academic, and the cultural and artistic materials.

Usually, the child is introduced first to some of the exercises of daily living. This is because they involve simple and precise tasks, which the young child has already observed adults perform in his home environment and therefore wishes to imitate. This desired imitation is intellectual in nature because it is based on the child's previous observation and knowledge. Because these exercises should have their roots in the child's immediate environment and culture, there can be no prescribed list of materials involved. The individual teacher must arrange her own exercises, using materials based on Montessori principles of beauty and simplicity, isolation of difficulty, proceeding from simple to complex, and indirect preparation. Although the exercises are skill-oriented in the sense that they involve washing a table or shining one's shoes, their purpose is not to master these tasks for their own sake. It is rather to aid the inner construction of discipline, organization, independence, and self-esteem through concentration on a precise and completed cycle of activity.

> The exercises of practical life are formative activities. They involve inspiration, repetition, and concentration on precise details. They take into account the natural impulses of special periods of childhood. Though for the moment the exercises have no merely practical aims, they are a work of adaptation to the environment. Such adaptation to the environment and efficient functioning therein is the very essence of a useful education.[51]

After inner discipline, confidence, and a conception of a full cycle of activity are initiated through the experience of daily living, the child is ready to be introduced to the sensorial materials. The aim of these materials is the education and refinement of the senses: visual, tactile, auditory, olfactory, gustatory, thermic, baric, sterognostic, and chromatic. This education is not undertaken so that the senses may function better; it is rather to assist the child in the development of his intelligence, which is dependent upon the organizing and categorizing of his sense perceptions into an inner mental order. Again, "it is exactly in the repetition of the exercises that the education of the senses consists."[52]

The academic materials are used to teach initially language, writing and reading, mathematics, geography, and science; they are a natural progression of the sensorial apparatus. They build upon the inner knowledge and construction the child has achieved through his previous manipulations on the concrete sensorial level and guide him to ever more abstract realms. The primary aim of the academic materials is again an inner one. It is not to store a quantity of knowledge in the child, but to satisfy his innate desire for learning and the development of his natural powers.

The cultural and artistic materials deal with self-expression and the communication of ideas. Like the daily-living experiences, many of these materials are by necessity rooted in the child's culture and environment and will therefore largely be determined by the individual teacher. Montessori did, however, designate some principles and equipment that are universally applicable. She felt the first step in music is to arouse the child's love and appreciation, and he therefore must be surrounded by good music in his environment. Rhythm and metrical exercises can then be developed. Activities such as "walking on the line" prepare the motor organs for rhythmical exercises. In this Montessori exercise, the children use a line drawn on the floor as a guide while they move very slowly, march, or run in rhythm with the music. This develops their sense of balance and control of movements of their hands and feet, which are necessary for dance, as well as being a preparation for music. A single musical phrase is repeated several times, or contrasting phrases are played, helping the child to develop his sensibility to music and capacity for interpreting differing rhythms into movement.

The next step is the study of harmony and melody. For this the child begins with very simple and primitive instruments suitable to his size and potentialities. He is given brief lessons on how to use the instruments, and is then permitted to use them freely. The writing and reading of music follows. The recognition of musical sounds has previously been taught by a sensorial exercise with musical bells which are paired and arranged according to pitch. Wooden discs shaped like notes with *do, re, mi,* etc., printed on them are placed at the foot of each bell according to its sound. In this way, even very young children are aware of notes as symbols of sounds. Montessori devised several wooden scale-boards with the movable note discs so that the children could teach themselves the notes in scale as well as treble and bass staffs. At this point, children can compose and read melodies using the note discs, and reproduce them on the bells. Older children develop musical notebooks similar to those used for writing.

Montessori gave no formal lessons in drawing or modeling. Instead, she concentrated on establishing a foundation within the child so he could be successful at them on his own initiative. The foundation for art and drawing is the same as that for writing: exercises that develop the muscles of the fingers and hands for holding pencils and making controlled movements. In addition, the development of the senses through the sensorial exercises aids the child's awareness and artistic appreciation of his environment.

> We do not teach drawing by drawing, however, but by providing the opportunity to prepare the instruments of expression. This I consider to be a real aid to free drawing, which, not being dreadful and incomprehensible, encourages the child to continue.[53]

The child's understanding of outline and color are also developed through special exercises, and the child learns how to mix paints before painting itself is introduced.

In sculpture also there are no formal lessons beyond an introduction to the materials. The child is left to work in free design. In some early Montessori schools a potter's wheel was used by the children, and diminutive bricks were baked in a furnace and used to construct walls and buildings, stimulating a beginning interest in architecture.[54]

Montessori's approach to the arts is a good example of her indirect approach to learning, which leads to increased creativity. The foundation is laid, and the child is then left free to do his own exploring. No one tries to "teach" him from his own finished work, for interfering in completed work always presents an obstacle to the child's development.

A sixth component of the Montessori method is the development of community life. The spontaneous creation of a community of children is one of the most remarkable outcomes of the Montessori approach. This development is aided by several key elements in the Montessori method. One of these is the sense of ownership and responsibility the children develop toward the classroom environment, largely because the classroom is indeed theirs and theirs alone. Everything in it is geared to their needs—physical, intellectual, and emotional. The teacher herself has no possessions there, not even a desk or chair of adult dimensions. The children are the key source of maintaining the daily order and care of the classroom. It is they who return the materials to the shelves, who polish the tables and care for the plants and animals.

A second element in the development of community life is the responsibility the children begin to feel for each other. Because the children for the most part work independently, particularly in the early years, many people do not understand how this social concern is developed in Montessori classrooms. Many people asked Montessori, "And how will the social sentiment be developed if each child works independently?" [55] but Montessori wondered that these same people could imagine that the traditional school setting, which regiments the children's actions and prevents them from helping one another in their work or even from freely communicating with each other, could possibly be considered as fostering social concern.

> We must therefore conclude that this system of regimentation in which the children do everything at the same moment, even to visiting the lavatory, is supposed to develop the social sentiment. The society of the child is therefore the antithesis of adult society, where sociability implies a free and well-bred

interchange of courtesies and mutual aid, although each individual attends to his own business.[56]

Montessori instead gave the children freedom in their social relations, limiting their actions only when they interfered with the rights of others. Through this freedom the child's natural interest in others and desire to help them grow spontaneously. Montessori found this concern and empathy for others was particularly apparent in the children's reactions to each other when someone disturbed the class. Instead of reprimanding the child who was misbehaving, they typically reacted with pity and "regarded his ill behavior as a mistake, tried to comfort him by telling him we were just as bad when we came!" [57] Again, when a child broke something, the children quickly came to help him clean up, and showed the same instinct to comfort.

A third element aiding the development of community life is the inclusion of children of differing ages in each class. The youngest class, for example, typically consists of twenty or twenty-five children of which one-third are three-year-olds, one-third four-year-olds, and one-third five-year-olds. At the end of the year, the oldest third moves on to the six–to–nine-year-old group, while another group of three-year-olds joins the three–to–six-year-old class. This means each child spends approximately three years in each class, with one-third of his companions being new each year. This emphasis on age mix is based in large part on the help older children are found to give spontaneously to the younger ones, as well as the inspiration and example they provide.

> There is a communication and harmony between the two that one seldom finds between the adult and the small child. . . . It is hard to believe how deep this atmosphere of protection and admiration becomes in practice.[58]

The older child is more sensitive to the nature and degree of help the young child needs.

They do not help one another as we do. . . . They respect one another's efforts, and give help only when necessary. This is very illuminating because it means they respect intuitively the essential need of childhood which is not to be helped unnecessarily.[59]

Although older children are allowed to teach the younger in a Montessori classroom, it should be noted that their own liberty is not infringed upon nor progress retarded when they do so.

People sometimes fear that if a child of five gives lessons, this will hold him back in his own progress. But, in the first place, he does not teach all the time and his freedom is respected. Secondly, teaching helps him to understand what he knows even better than before. He has to analyze and rearrange his little store of knowledge before he can pass it on. So his sacrifice does not go unrewarded.[60]

Not only did Montessori mix the ages of the children in each class; the classes themselves are ideally separated not by solid walls but by "waist-high partitions; and there is always easy access from one classroom to the next . . . one can always go for an intellectual walk." [61] Thus the younger children are inspired by exposure to the possibilities of their future, and older children can retreat temporarily to a simpler and less challenging environment when they have such a need.

Although Montessori did not emphasize the collective attention of a group of children at one time, she did feel collective education had its place as a preparation for life. "For also, in life, it sometimes happens that we must all remain seated and quiet; when, for example, we attend a concert or a lecture. And we know that even to us, as grown people, this costs no little sacrifice." [62] She did, therefore, after individual discipline had been established, assist children in accomplishing a collective order. She did this principally by helping the children to be aware of group order when it was achieved, rather than by forcing them to remain in attentive order while receiving instructions. "To make them understand the idea, without calling their attention too forcibly to the practice, to have them assimilate a principle of collective order— that is the important thing." [63] One technique Montessori devised for reinforcing this principle of collective order is the "silence game." She began this game by drawing the children's attention to how silent and immobile she could be, and inviting them to imitate this absolute silence.

They watch me in amazement when I stand in the middle of the room, so quietly that it is really as if "I were not." Then they strive to imitate me, and to do even better. I call attention here and there to a foot that moves, almost inadvertently. The attention of the child is called to every part of his body in an anxious eagerness to attain immobility.[64]

Sometimes whispered instructions are given to individual children to perform certain acts as quietly as possible. The delight the children show in this silence game is intriguing. They seem to enjoy the feeling of a common achievement in which each plays an integral part; moreover, "The children, after they had made the effort necessary to maintain silence, enjoyed the sensation, took pleasure in the silence itself." [65]

The Montessori teacher who is responsible for these six components of the prepared environment for the child should perhaps not be called a teacher at all. Montessori called her a "directress." This translation from the Italian still does not convey the role the Montessori teacher plays in the child's life, however, for her approach is actually an indirect rather than a direct one. It is similar to that used in therapy, where the goal is not to impose the will of one person on another, but to set free the individual's own potential for constructive self-development. In this further discussion of the Montessori teacher, it would be helpful to keep in mind this distinction between the teacher as understood in the traditional sense and the teacher of the Montessori approach.

It should also be kept in mind that, although the teacher

is here referred to in the feminine gender, male teachers, even for three-year-old children, are very much a part of Montessori tradition and an integral part of any classroom's success. In fact, one of the advantages of the team-teaching approach of Montessori is the possibility it presents for having both male and female teachers in the classroom.

It has already been said that the teacher must be a growing person, one who is involved in ever striving toward his or her own potential. In order to be involved in this process of becoming, a person must have a realistic knowledge of self and be capable of reflecting objectively on one's own capabilities and behavior. This development of self-knowledge is an essential first step toward becoming a successful Montessori teacher.

> The real preparation for education is the study of one's self. The training of the teacher who is to help life is something far more than the learning of ideas. It includes the training of character; it is a preparation of the spirit.[66]

This interior preparation requires guidance from without. "To discover defects that have become part and parcel of his [the teacher's] consciousness requires help and instruction." [67] Montessori felt that the adult, by examining himself in this way, would begin to understand what it is that stands in the way between adult and child.

> The adult has not understood the child or the adolescent and is therefore in continual strife with him. The remedy is not that the adult should learn something intellectually, or complete a deficient culture. He must find a different starting point. The adult must find in himself the hitherto unknown error that prevents him from seeing the child as he is.[68]

Montessori believed that this error was the adult's assumption that the child is an empty vessel waiting to be filled with our knowledge and experience rather than a being who must develop his own potential for life.

> The adult has become egocentric in relation to the child, not egotistic, but egocentric. Thus he considers everything from the standpoint of its reference to himself, and so misunderstands the child. It is this point of view that leads to a consideration of the child as an empty being, which the adult must fill by his own endeavors, as an inert and incapable being for whom everything must be done, as a being without an inner guide, whom the adult must guide step by step from without. Finally, the adult acts as though he were the child's creator, and considers good and evil in the child's actions from the standpoint of relation to himself. . . . And in adopting such an attitude, which unconsciously cancels the child's personality, the adult feels a conviction of zeal, love and sacrifice.[69]

Adults must aim to diminish their egocentric and authoritarian attitude toward the child and adopt a passive attitude in order to aid in his development. They must approach children with humility, recognizing their role as a secondary one.

> The adult must recognize that he must take second place, endeavor all he can to understand the child, and to support and help him in the development of his life. This should be the aim of mother and teacher. If the child's personality is to be helped to develop, since the child is the weaker, the adult with his stronger personality must hold himself in check, and, taking his lead from the child, feel proud if he can understand and follow him.[70]

To understand and follow the child, the Montessori teacher must develop the desire and ability to observe him.[71]

> The teacher must bring not only the capacity, but the desire to observe natural phenomena. In our system, she must become a passive, much more than an active, influence, and her passivity shall be composed of anxious scientific curiosity, and of absolute respect for the phenomenon which she wishes to

observe. The teacher must understand and feel her position of observer: the activity must lie in the phenomenon.[72]

The ability to hold observation of life in such esteem does not come readily to the adult.

This idea, that life acts of itself, and that in order to study it, to divine its secrets or to direct its activity, it is necessary to observe it and to understand it without intervening—this idea, I say, is very difficult for anyone to assimilate and to put into practice.[73]

In order to do this, "a habit . . . must be developed by practice. . . . To observe it is necessary to be 'trained.'"[74] This training for scientific observation is not a matter primarily of mechanical skill, however.

It is my belief that the thing which we should cultivate in our teachers is more the spirit than the mechanical skill of the scientist; that is, the direction of the preparation should be toward the spirit rather than toward the mechanism.[75]

This spirit has three aspects. One is an interest in humanity: "The interest in humanity to which we wish to educate the teacher must be characterized by the intimate relationship between the observer and the individual to be observed."[76] Further, it is an ability to see children as individuals, each unique and unlike any other.

Now, child life is not an abstraction; it is the life of individual children. There exists only one real biological manifestation: the living individual; and toward single individuals, one by one observed, education must direct itself.[77]

Finally, it is based on the faith that the child can and will reveal himself, and that through this revelation the teacher will discover what his role must be. "From the child itself he [the teacher] will learn how to perfect himself as an educator." [78]

It is not outward growth and activities the teacher is to watch for, but the internal coordination that these may be manifesting.

> The important point is, not that the embryo grows, but that it coordinates. "Growth" comes through and by order, which also makes life possible. An embryo which grows without coordinating its internal organs is not vital. Here we have not only the impulse, but the mystery of life. The evolution of internal order is the essential condition for the realization of vital existence in a life which possesses the impulse to exist. Now the sum of the phenomena indicated in the "guide to psychological observation" actually represents the evolution of spiritual order in the child.[79]

Montessori then gives the following "guide to psychological observation" of the child in three key areas: his work, his conduct, and the development of his will and self-discipline to include voluntary obedience.

> WORK—Note when a child begins to occupy himself for any length of time upon a task.
>
> What the task is and how long he continues working at it (slowness in completing it and repetition of the same exercise).
>
> His individual peculiarities in applying himself to particular tasks.
>
> To what tasks he applies himself during the same day, and with how much perseverance.
>
> If he has periods of spontaneous industry, and for how many days these periods continue.
>
> How he manifests a desire to progress.
>
> What tasks he chooses in their sequence, working at them steadily.
>
> Persistence in a task in spite of stimuli in his environment which would tend to distract his attention.
>
> If after deliberate interruption he resumes the task from which his attention was distracted.

CONDUCT—Note the state of order or disorder in the acts of the child.

His disorderly actions.

Note if changes of behavior take place during the development of the phenomena of work.

Note whether during the establishment of ordered actions there are:

> crises of joy;
> intervals of serenity;
> manifestations of affection.

The part the child takes in the development of his companions.

OBEDIENCE—Note if the child responds to the summons when he is called.

Note if and when the child begins to take part in the work of others with an intelligent effort.

Note when obedience to a summons becomes regular.

Note when obedience to orders becomes established.

Note when the child obeys eagerly and joyously.

Note the relation of the various phenomena of obedience in their degrees

> (a) to the development of work;
> (b) to the changes of conduct.[80]

In addition to her role as an observer, the teacher serves as the preparer and communicator of the environment for the child. The designing and caring for the environment requires a major portion of the Montessori teacher's time and energy, reflecting the dominant role Montessori gave to it in the educative process.

> The teacher's first duty is to watch over the environment, and this takes precedence over all the rest. Its influence is indirect, but unless it be well done thre will be no effective and permanent results of any kind, physical, intellectual or spiritual.[81]

She is responsible for the atmosphere and order of the classroom, the display and condition of materials, and the programming of activities, challenges, and changes of pace to meet each child's individual needs. Particular emphasis is placed on keeping the materials in excellent order: "All the apparatus is to be kept meticulously in order, beautiful and shining, in perfect condition. Nothing may be missing, so that to the child it always seems new, complete and ready for use." [82]

The Montessori teacher also serves as the exemplar in the environment, thus inspiring the children's own development. This is an important reason for her to strive for flexibility, warmth, and love of life, as well as understanding and respect for self. She must be as physically attractive as possible, for in this way she attracts the children's attention and respect.

> The teacher also must be attractive, tidy and clean, calm and dignified [for her] appearance is the first step to gaining the child's confidence and respect. . . . So, care for one's own person must form part of the environment in which the child lives; the teacher, herself, is the most vital part of his world.[83]

Lest this idea of serving as a model for young children be interpreted as a requirement for perfection, it is important to realize that Montessori had no such expectations for her teachers. She advised them instead to be realistic about their shortcomings, knowing that in doing so they would be helping their children to develop a healthy attitude toward their own mistakes.

> It becomes apparent that everyone makes mistakes. This is one of life's realities, and to admit it is already to have taken a great step forward. If we are to tread the narrow path of truth and keep our hold upon reality, we have to agree that all of us can err; otherwise we should all be perfect. So it is well to cultivate a friendly feeling toward error, to treat it as a companion inseparable from our lives, as something having a purpose which it truly has.[84]

And again,

> errors made by adults have a certain interest, and children sympathize with them, but in a wholly detached way. It be-

comes for them one of the natural aspects of life, and the fact that we can all make mistakes stirs a deep feeling of affection in their hearts; it is one more reason for the union between mother and child. Mistakes bring us closer and make us better friends. Fraternity is born more easily on the road of error than on that of perfection.[85]

The teacher is also the link that puts the child in touch with the environment. The child is totally dependent on this help from the teacher: "The child's one hope lies in his interpreter." [86] In particular, he cannot gain full benefit from the learning material in the environment without the teacher's inspiration and guidance.

I felt this, intuitively, and believed that not the didactic material, but my voice which called to them, awakened the children, and encouraged them to use the didactic material, and through it, to educate themselves. . . . Without such inspiration [encouragement, comfort, love, and respect], the most perfect external stimulus may pass unobserved.[87]

The role of communicator is a delicate one, and the teacher must be careful not to overdo her part.

There is a period of life extraordinarily open to suggestion—the period of infancy—when consciousness is in process of formation and sensibility toward external factors is in a creative state. . . . We noticed in our schools that if in showing a child how to do anything we did so with too much enthusiasm, or performed the movements with too much energy or excessive accuracy, we quenched the child's capacity of judging and acting according to his own personality.[88]

Montessori teachers function as a team, with two teachers per class, usually an experienced teacher and an assistant. This team approach gives the child an option as to which adult he prefers to relate to at any given time; but more important it means that the teachers are not operating in a vacuum, without benefit of feedback from another adult. At the end of each day, they discuss the progress of each child and exchange ideas and observations.

The Montessori teacher must give a good deal of her time to family and community relations. Montessori viewed the child as a member of a family—not as an isolated individual—and one whose most formative life experiences take place outside the classroom. She had no illusions that, without close communication and cooperation with the parents, the school hours, even though they lasted a full day, could have a transforming effect for the child. The regulations posted on the walls for the first Casa dei Bambini demonstrate clearly how seriously Montessori considered this matter. "The mothers are obliged to send their children to the 'Children's House' clean, and to cooperate with the Directress in the educational work." [89] If the parents did not cooperate, their child was returned to them.

> If the child shows through its conversation that the educational work of the school is being undermined by the attitude taken in his home, he will be sent back to his parents, to teach them thus how to take advantage of their good opportunities. . . . In other words, the parents must learn to deserve the benefit of having within the house the great advantage of a school for their little ones. [90]

Each mother was to

> go at least once a week to confer with the directress, giving an account of her child, and accepting any helpful advice which the directress may be able to give. . . . The directress is always at the disposition of the mothers, and her life, as a cultured and educated person, is a constant example to the inhabitants of the house, for she is obliged to live in the tenement and to be therefore a cohabitant with the families of all her pupils. This is a fact of immense importance. [91]

This close contact, and the fact they paid part of its

expenses, helped the parents feel a special proprietorship toward the school. The classroom was a "property of the collectivity . . . maintained by a portion of the rent they pay." The mothers were permitted to "go at any hour of the day to watch, to admire, or to meditate upon the life there." [92] By thus establishing an open relationship with the home environment, Montessori hoped to influence the social background of future generations.

> Man is . . . a social product, and the social environment of individuals in the process of education is the home. Scientific pedagogy will seek in vain to better the new generation if it does not succeed in influencing also the environment within which this new generation grows! I believe . . . we have solved the problem of being able to modify directly the environment of the new generation.[93]

In addition to maintaining as close a contact as possible with the children's parents and family life, the Montessori teacher has an important role to play as an interpreter of Montessori aims to the community at large. There is a great demand to know more about Montessori education on the part of parents and teachers, and Montessori teachers must be capable and willing to meet their requests for lectures, demonstrations, and visits. They do this as a part of their commitment to the child and his education, a commitment that extends beyond their own classrooms.

What is a classroom based on the freedom and structure of a Montessori environment, where the teachers follow the indirect approach of the Montessori method, like? It is a living place, full of children in search of themselves and their world. There is a feeling of total involvement as children explore and discover, sometimes with materials on rugs on the floor or on tables; sometimes alone, sometimes together. There is much movement, self-initiated socializing, and casual interchange between children and between child and teacher.

The teacher is hard to find. There is no teacher's desk, nor anything else in the room to cast her in the role of the "captain at the helm," as in many traditional classrooms. She is likely to be on a rug on the floor, or at a child-sized table, giving full attention to one individual child at a time. Careful observation of her will show she is constantly on the move in a quiet way, as she goes from child to child and seeks to be alert to the needs and actions of all.

There is no formal schedule chopping the day into small pieces; there is only the obligation to begin and end the day at the regular times, or, if the class is housed in a larger school, to comply with the demands of this larger environment. Actually, close observation will show that the children set themselves a kind of flexible schedule, varying the choice and pace of their activities. Contrary to traditional thought, they do not choose the hardest work when they first arrive and are considered "freshest." Instead, they consistently choose easy work at first, and gradually work up to a very challenging endeavor—"the great work" of the day, as Montessori called it—later in the morning.

However, it takes careful preparation and time for a beginning Montessori class to reach the optimal functioning of the class described, and parents and teachers alike are discouraged if they expect such a class of twenty or thirty children to appear in full bloom immediately. Time and experience are necessary before the children can develop the inner discipline required to utilize the freedom of the Montessori classroom effectively. In an already functioning class, where two-thirds of the children have had this opportunity in the previous year, the younger third entering the class for the first time readily develop such discipline through imitation of the older ones and special attention from the teacher, particularly when they are admitted a few at a time. When a class is first begun, there is no established community of children, and the teacher alone must "show the way to discipline." [94]

If discipline had already arrived our work would hardly be needed; the child's instinct would be a safe enough guide enabling him to deal with every difficulty. But the child of three, when he first comes to school, is a fighter on the verge of being vanquished; he has already adopted a defensive attitude which masks his deeper energies. The higher energies, which could guide him to a disciplined peace and a divine wisdom, are asleep.[95]

To the extent that this is true of individual children, the teacher

must call to them, wake them up, by her voice and thought. . . . Before she draws aside to leave the children free, she watches and directs them for some time, preparing them in a negative sense, that is to say, by eliminating their uncontrolled movements.[96]

She does this by introducing a series of preparatory exercises that help the children to concentrate on reality and control of movement. They may consist of arranging chairs and tables in proper places without making any noise, moving about the room on tiptoe, whispering instructions to carry out, or practicing total silence. It is necessary to charm the children in order to carry out these exercises successfully. "Sometimes I use a word easily misunderstood: the teacher must be seductive, she must entice the children." [97]

Any child who cannot be reached in this way must be dealt with more directly.

If at this stage there is some child who persistently annoys the others, the most practical thing to do is to interrupt him. It is true that we have said, and repeated often enough, that when a child is absorbed in his work, one must refrain from interfering, so as not to interrupt his cycle of activity or prevent its free expansion; nevertheless, the right technique now is just the opposite; it is to break the flow of the disturbing activity. The interruption may take the form of any kind of exclamation, or in showing a special and affectionate interest in the troublesome child.[98]

Gradually some of the exercises of daily living are introduced, and eventually, little by little, the didactic materials. A period of apparent order follows, but at first

the children keep going from one thing to another. They do each thing once; then they go and fetch something else. . . . The appearance of discipline which may be obtained is actually very fragile, and the teacher, who is constantly warding off a disorder which she feels to be "in the air," is kept in a state of tension.[99]

At this point the teacher must both supervise the children and also begin individual lessons showing the precise use of the materials, as described earlier in the Fundamental Lesson, but she must be careful to keep watch over the activities of the other children as well. Now it is that the children begin, one by one, to show the phenomena of repetition and concentration that indicates self-discipline has begun. The teacher

sees the children becoming ever more independent in choosing their work and in the richness of their powers of expression. Sometimes their progress seems miraculous. . . . This, however, is the moment in which the child has the greatest need of her authority.[100]

After completing something important to them, "instinct leads [the children] to submit their work to an external authority so as to be sure they are following the right path." [101]

A last stage is accomplished when the child no longer seeks the approval of authority after each step.

He will go on piling up finished work of which the others know nothing, obeying merely the need to produce and perfect the fruits of his industry. What interests him is finishing his work, not to have it admired, nor to treasure it up as his own property.[102]

It is now that inner discipline has been firmly established, and the teacher must be most careful not to interfere with the child in any way. "Praise, help, or even a look, may be enough to interrupt him, or destroy the activity. It seems a strange thing to say, but this can happen even if the child merely becomes aware of being watched."[103] Even when several children wish to use the same materials at once, the teacher is not to interfere unless asked.

> But even to solve these problems, one should not interfere unless asked; the children will solve them by themselves. . . . The teacher's skill in not interfering comes with practice, like everything else, but it never comes easily [for] even to help can be a source of pride.[104]

In such a classroom, the real education of the children can begin, for they have arrived at self-discipline, and have thus achieved freedom for their own development. This is the goal toward which all Montessori philosophy and method are aimed, and in which Montessori found such hope for mankind.

1. "by spring of the first year, the children were happy and working hard"

2. "mental development *must* be connected with movement" [the brown stair]

3. "children work for the sake of process; adults work to achieve an end result"

4. "ours live always in an active community"

5. "between six and nine, then, he is capable of building the academic and artistic skills essential for a life of fulfillment"

6. "the children are, therefore, free to move about the classroom at will—ideally to an outside environment . . . as well as inside the classroom"

7. "the first essential for the child's development is concentration"

8. "the materials progress from simple to more complex design and usage" [the smaller numerical rods]

9. "the materials begin as concrete expressions of an idea" [the geometric solids]

10. "the control of error guides the child in his use of the materials and permits him to recognize his own mistakes" [the multiplication chart board]

11. "the inner construction of discipline, organization, independence, and self-esteem"

12. "to assist the child in the development of his intelligence" [the trinomial cube]

13. "to satisfy his innate desire for learning"

14. "there is a communication and harmony between the two"

15. "[adults] must approach children with humility, recognizing their role as a secondary one"

16. "the intimate relationship between the observer and the individual to be observed" [the musical bells]

17. "the control of movement and eye–hand coordination"

18. "in preparation for writing movements and holding a pencil" [the metal insets]

19. "a continuous encouragement of self-expression and communication" [a card matching game]

20. "the Metal Insets complete the possibility for an explosion into writing"

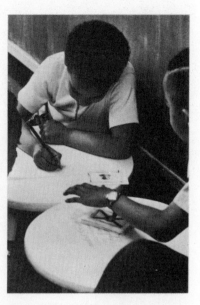

21. "writing develops as naturally as oral language did in an earlier period"

22. "the more knowledge that is made available to the child, the more he is stimulated to explore language" [the object game]

23. "the intent is only to give the key that different words do different things" [the farm]

24. "to experience the thrill of discovering the unknown for himself"

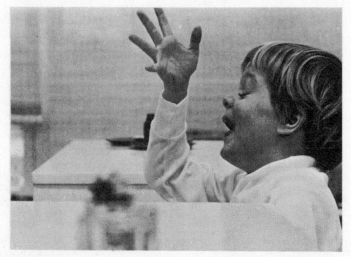

25. "freedom . . . to communicate and share his discoveries with others at will"

26. "a good example of her indirect approach to learning, which leads to increased creativity"

4

Montessori
and Parents

MONTESSORI BELIEVED that an important mission of parents was to work for the establishment of the child's rightful place in society. The child's needs should come before all others, for, if mankind is to progress, it must be through the child. However, instead of putting the child first, our society is spending its money on unnecessary luxuries and technological improvements, polluting the environment and overpopulating the earth.

> The greatest crime that society is committing is that of wasting the money it should spend for its children, of dissipating it to destroy them and itself. . . . When wasteful society has urgent need of money, it takes it from the schools and especially from the infant schools that shelter the seeds of human life. . . . This is humanity's worst crime and greatest error. Society does not even perceive that it destroys twice over when it uses its money for instruments of destruction; it destroys by not enabling to live and it destroys by bringing death. And the two are one and the same error.[1]

Parents have an important mission: "They alone can and must save their children. . . . Their consciences must feel the force of the mission entrusted to them by nature . . . for in their hands lies positively the future of humanity, life."[2]

Montessori saw that parents in our society are failing to do this. Instead they are preoccupied with

> struggle, efforts at adaptation, and labor for outward conquests. The events of the world of men all converge on conquest and production, as if there were nothing else to be considered. Human effort clashes and is broken in competition. . . . If the adult considers the child, he does so with the logic he brings to bear on his own like. He sees in the child a different and useless creature and he keeps him at a distance; or else through what is called education, he endeavors to draw him prematurely and directly into the forms of his own life. . . . The adult exhibits before them his own perfection, his own maturity, his own historical example, calling upon the child to imitate him.[3]

As a scientist, Montessori was much aware of the radical changes lower forms of nature undergo to protect and nurture their young, and was puzzled that man himself did not exhibit these same instincts to the same degree.

> How can we explain such a mistaken conception in the loftiest, furthest evolved being, gifted with a mind of his own? Is the denominator of his environment, the creature full of power, able to work with an immeasurable superiority over all other living things?
> Yet he the architect, the builder, the producer, the transformer of his environment, does less for his child than the bees, than the insects, and any other creature.[4]

In addition to fighting for the rights of the child in society, the parent holds primary responsibility for the life and development of his own children. Although Montessori advocated formal schooling for children at a much earlier age than previous educators, she gave the sole responsibility for the beginning years of the child's life to the parent. The earliest Montessori usually considered placing a child in a school environment was at the age of two and a half, and more customarily at three. This meant the child would be in his home environment, with his parents in charge of his activities, for the first three years of life—the years Montessori considered more important than any others for the child's development.

> The development of the child during the first three years after birth is unequalled in intensity and importance by any period that precedes or follows in the whole life of the child. . . . If we consider the transformations, adaptations, achievements, and conquest of the environment during the first period of life from zero to three years, it is functionally a longer period than all the following periods put together from three years until death. For this reason, these three years may be considered to be as long as a whole life.[5]

The child's needs during this period are "so imperious that they cannot be ignored without harmful consequences ever after." [6]

Montessori particularly emphasized the importance of the mother to the child, including the period immediately after birth. Since the child is passing from one form of existence to another, "in no other period of man's life will he find a like occasion of struggle and conflict, and hence of suffering." [7] Because birth is such a "dramatic episode" in the child's life, Montessori felt it was essential for the child to "remain [in the first few days] as much as possible in contact with his mother." This physical closeness aids

> the child's adaptation to the world . . . because there is a special bond uniting mother and child, almost like a magnetic attraction.
>
> The mother radiates invisible forces to which the child is accustomed, and they are a help to him in the difficult days of adjustment.
>
> We may say that the child has merely changed his position in regard to her: he is now outside her body instead of inside. But everything else remains the same and the communion between them still exists.[8]

Although Montessori emphasized the parent's role and the family unit in the child's early life, she did not approve of the concept of the family as an isolated unit. She felt this isolation divided men and kept them from discovering their true condition of brotherhood.

> Why do men isolate themselves one from the other, and why does every family group shut itself up with a feeling of isolation and of repugnance toward other groups? The family does not isolate itself to find enjoyment in itself, but to separate itself from others. These barriers are not built to defend love. The family barriers are closed, insurmountable, more powerful than the walls of the house. So, too, are the barriers separating classes and nations.[9]

In keeping with this concept of closer communication between families, Montessori advocated what she called a "socializing" of a mother's work. By this she meant a cooperation for mutual benefit, such as society had at that time accomplished in the fields of transportation through the use of streetcars, in electricity through street lights, and in communication through the telephone. She had established her "Children's Houses" in apartment buildings, giving mothers who needed or wished the opportunity to leave the children in a beneficial environment that they themselves supported and paid for. Montessori also foresaw a time when there might be an infirmary in the apartment building as well, and a kitchen program where, if desired, a dinner could be ordered in the morning and delivered, perhaps by dumbwaiter, in the evening. Thus liberated from many of the chores of the past, the "new woman" was to be "like man, an individual, a free human being, a social worker; and, like man, she shall seek blessing and repose within the house." [10]

Montessori did not consider the parents' responsibility for the child's early years to rest on the fact that they had produced him and therefore were entitled to complete control over him. On the contrary, it is the child who must produce

himself; the authority of the parents over him is legitimate
only insofar as the parents are helpful to him in this task.
"The parent's role is that of a guardian, not a creator." [11]

> What the mother brings forth is the baby, but it is the baby
> who produces the man. . . . To recognize this great work of
> the child does not mean to diminish the parents' authority.
> Once they can persuade themselves not to be themselves the
> builders, but merely to act as collaborators in the building
> process, they become much better able to carry out their real
> duties. . . . Thus, the authority of parents does not come from
> a dignity standing on its own feet, but it comes from the help
> they are able to give their children. The truly great authority
> and dignity of parents rests solely upon this.[12]

The role of the parent is to "care for, and keep awake, the
guide within every child." [13]

The child, then, is given his own powers for development,
and, if the parent is to be helpful, he must try to learn from
the child himself what he must do.

> Nature has given to this new person [the child] its laws, and all
> that takes place is not in our hands. Not that we cannot help;
> we can and do, but we had the idea that it was we adults who
> built him, that we must do everything for this little child
> instead of seeing how much he can give to us. . . . In the child
> is much knowledge, much wisdom. If we do not profit from
> it, is only because of neglect on our part to become humble
> and to see the wonder of this soul and learn what the child can
> teach.[14]

Erik Erikson, the noted psychoanalyst and an early Montes-
sorian, emphasizes this growth which must take place as part
of parenthood:

> Parents who are faced with the development of a number of
> children must constantly live up to a challenge. They must
> develop with them. . . . Babies control and bring up their
> families as much as they are controlled by them.[15]

If parents are to learn and grow with their children, they must develop the power to observe them, to enjoy them, and to accept them. All of these depend upon a willingness to adopt the slower pace of the child and to trust his inner powers. It is difficult for the adult, who must attain his goals in the most efficient manner possible, not to interrupt the child's slower efforts.

> Seeing the child make great efforts to perform a totally useless action, or one so futile that he himself could perform it in an instant and far better, he [the adult] is tempted to help. . . . The adult is irritated not only by the fact that the child is trying to perform an action when there is no need, but also by his different rhythm, his different manner of moving.[16]

The adult is therefore constantly hurrying and pushing the child. Dorothy Canfield Fisher, an American novelist and mother who went to Europe to study under Dr. Montessori, describes this rushing of children vividly in her book *The Montessori Mother*. She says that, in writing of her own children, she came to realize she had been "dragging them head-long on a Cook's tour through life." [17] Montessori believed,

> The adult must be always calm and act slowly so that all the details of his action may be clear to the child who is watching.
> If the adult abandons himself to his usual quick, powerful rhythms, then instead of inspiring he may engrave his own personality on the child's, and substitute himself for the child by suggestion.[18]

To ensure his child's positive development, the parent must prepare the proper home environment for him. The child's need is for a home that is a place

> of beauty . . . that is not contaminated or determined by any outward need . . . where man feels the need to suspend and forget his usual characteristics, where he perceives that the essential thing that maintains life is something other than

struggle . . . that to oppress others is not the secret of survival or the important thing in life . . . where therefore a surrender of self seems truly life-giving.[19]

Such a harboring environment is a boon to the adult; it is a necessity for the child if he is to develop to his fullest potential, because of the different relationship of the child to his environment. The child doesn't just live in his environment; it becomes a part of him.

He absorbs the life going on about him and becomes one with it. . . . The child's impressions are so profound that a biological or psycho-chemical change takes place, by which his mind ends by resembling the environment itself.[20]

Because it was his first contact with the world, Montessori felt parents should take great care "of all the conditions surrounding the newborn babe, so that he will not be repelled and develop regressive tendencies but feel attracted to the new world into which he has come." The environment for the first few days should simulate the mother's womb. "There must not be too much contrast, as regards warmth, light, noise, with his conditions before birth, where, in his mother's womb, there was perfect silence, darkness, and an even temperature." [21] After this initial transitory period, Montessori was much against the isolation of the baby from the social life about him.

Actually, the baby's natural environment is the world, everything that lies round about him. To learn a language he must live with those who speak it, otherwise he will not be able to. If he is to acquire special mental powers he must live with people who constantly use those powers. The manners, habits, and customs of his group can only be derived from mingling with those who possess them. [If the child is] left alone, and made to sleep as much as possible, as if he were ill [or] shut away in a nursery with no other companion than a nurse . . . his normal growth and development are arrested.[22]

The child must be allowed to take part in the parents' life in spite of the problems this entails. "Notwithstanding the many objections that can be made, it has to be said that if we want to help the child we must keep him with us, so that he can see what we do and hear what we say." [23] In this respect, Montessori felt other peoples of the world were more enlightened in their rearing of children than those in Western countries. In other cultures, babies are constantly with their mothers and go everywhere with them. Montessori believed that it was because of this they seldom cry, whereas

> the crying of children is a problem in Western countries. . . . The child is bored. He is being mentally starved, kept prisoner in a confined space offering nothing but frustration to the exercise of his powers. The only remedy is to release him from solitude, and let him join in social life.[24]

As the baby becomes older, his growing independence sets up an increasing conflict between the parents' wishes and the child's needs.

> The conflict between the grownup and the child begins when the child has reached a point where he can do things on his own. Earlier no one can wholly prevent the child from seeing and hearing, that is, from making a sensory conquest of his world. . . . But when the child grows active, walks, touches things, it is quite another thing. Grownups, however much they love a child, feel an irresistible instinct to defend themselves from him. It is an unconscious feeling of fear of disturbance by an unreasoning creature, combined with a proprietary sense where objects are concerned that might be dirtied or spoiled.[25]

Thus it is the parent, even though he truly loves his child, who is in danger of becoming the child's first enemy in his struggle for life. This occurs because the parent fails to understand that, unlike himself, the child is in the process of becoming.

This is the first contest of the man who enters the world: he has to struggle with his parents, with those who have given him life. And this occurs because his infant life is "different" from that of his parents; the child has to form himself, whereas his parents are already formed.[26]

When the child develops the ability to walk, the parent continues to interfere with his growth, both because he feels it is necessary for the child's safety and because the adult does not wish to—or is not capable of—reducing his pace to that of the child.

We know that the child starts walking with an irresistible impetus and courage. He is bold, even rash; he is a soldier who hurls himself to victory regardless of risk. And for this reason the adult surrounds him with protective restrictions, which are so many obstacles; he is enclosed within a rail, or strapped in a perambulator, in which he will make his outings even when his legs are already sturdy.

This happens because a child's step is much shorter than that of a grownup, and he has less staying-power for long walks. And the grownup will not give up his own pace.[27]

As the child who now walks about begins to explore the objects in his environment, the adult's way of life is further threatened. As a result, instead of welcoming this new activity, the parent seeks to stifle it.

The first stretching out of those tiny hands toward things, the impetus of a movement that represents the effort of the ego to penetrate the world, should fill the adult observer with wonder and reverence. And instead man is afraid of those tiny hands as they stretch out to the valueless and insignificant objects within their reach; he sets out to defend these objects against the child. He is constantly repeating, "Don't touch!" just as he repeats, "Sit still! Be quiet!" [28]

The child wants to handle and touch all those objects he sees others about him using.

[He] is not just running, or jumping, or handling things aimlessly, or simply displacing them so as to create disorder, or destroy them. Constructive movement finds its urge in actions that the child has seen performed by others. The actions he tries to imitate are always those that mean the handling or the use of something, with which the child tries to perform the actions he has seen performed by adults. Therefore these activities are associated with the usages of his various domestic or social surroundings. The child will want to sweep and wash up, or wash clothes, pour out water, or wash and dress himself, brush his own hair.[29]

When the child inevitably wishes to explore objects that belong to others, a substitution can be made.

It goes without saying that there will often be war between the grownup and the child over these too alluring objects which are so eminently tabooed because they belong to mamma's dressing table or daddy's writing-desk or the drawing room furniture. And often the result is "naughtiness." But the child does not want that particular bottle, or that ink-stand; he would be satisfied with things made for him, allowing him to practice the same movements.[30]

Adults can readily understand that it is important to allow the child to explore his environment, but it is rare that they are able to permit it freely:

The idea of leaving the baby free to act is one that is easily understood, but which in practice encounters complicated obstacles deeply rooted in the adult mind. Often a grownup who will wish to leave the child free to touch and move things will be unable to resist vague impulses which end by mastering him.[31]

In his early explorations of his environment, the child is seeking to establish his independence through mastering his surroundings. It is up to the parent to permit the necessary exploration and also to arrange the environment so that the child can learn to do things for himself. In her schools Montessori gave the child

> objects which he can handle by himself and which he can learn to master. This principle can be applied, and must be applied, in the child's own home. From the earliest possible age the child must be provided with things which may help him to do things by himself.[32]

This means that everything the child must use in taking care of himself must be in proportion to his size and ability; the hook to hang his clothes on; the places where he washes and brushes his teeth, where he hangs his towel, where he throws soiled clothes, where there is a broom and dustpan of his own size for cleaning up, where he sits, where he eats—all must be suitable for a child's use. His clothes particularly should be chosen for the ease with which he will be able to get in and out of them on his own.

Montessori was concerned that a child might be waited on unnecessarily and, therefore, not develop the independence vital to a full life. She wrote about servants performing this function. Today it is more likely to be the mother acting in the role of servant, but the principle is still applicable.

> In an age of civilization where servants exist, the concept of that form of life which is independence cannot take root or develop freely. . . . Our servants are not our dependents, rather it is we who are dependent upon them. . . . In reality, he who is served is limited. . . . Who does not know that to teach a child to feed himself, to wash and dress himself, is a much more tedious and difficult work, calling for infinitely greater patience, than feeding, washing, and dressing the child one's self? But the former is the work of an educator, the latter is the easy and inferior work of a servant. . . . These dangers should be presented to the parents of the privileged social classes, if their children are to use independently and for right the special power which is theirs. Needless help is an actual hindrance to the development of natural forces.[33]

Not only do the natural abilities of the child remain undeveloped if he is waited on unnecessarily; negative characteristics
emerge.

> The peril of servilism and independence lies not only in that
> "useless consuming of life," which leads to helplessness, but in
> the development of individual traits which indicate all too
> plainly a regrettable perversion and degeneration of the normal
> man. . . . The domineering habit develops side by side with
> helplessness. It is the outward sign of the state of feeling of
> him who conquers through the work of others.[34]

The whole trend of our culture toward less and less work
for ourselves alarmed Montessori. For her, to be alive is to be
active.

> Everything in the living world is active. Life is activity at its
> peak, and it is only through activity that the perfectionments
> of life can be sought and gained. The social aspirations handed
> down to us by past generations, the ideal of minimum working
> hours, of having others to work for us, of idleness ever more
> complete . . . these aspirations are signs of regression in the
> person who was not helped in the first days of his life to adapt
> to his environment, and who therefore feels antipathy toward
> it, toward exertion. His was the type of childhood with a liking
> for being helped and waited on.[35]

Montessori felt that the adult in our culture is unprepared
to recognize and accept the young child's desire for work and,
therefore, is not only amazed when it appears, but refuses to
allow its expression. He instead tries to force the child to play
continuously. Adults must learn to recognize the child's instinct for work and cooperate with it.

> We must also reject the idea that the joy of a child is in being
> forced to play all the time or the major part of the day.
>   The foundation of education must be based on the follow-
> ing facts: that the joy of the child is in accomplishing things
> great for his age; that the real satisfaction of the child is to

give maximum effort to the task in hand; that happiness consists in well-directed activity of body and mind in the way of excellence; that strength of mind and body and spirit is acquired by exercise and experience.[36]

Erik Erikson describes the child's need for work and accomplishment as the first "infantile steps toward identity" and realistic self-esteem.

In this children cannot be fooled by empty praise and condescending encouragement. . . . Ego identity gains real strength only from wholehearted and consistent recognition of real accomplishment—i.e., of achievement that has meaning in our culture.

Our culture, in contrast to others, impedes the child in this task. Erikson cites the childhood of the Papago Indian in Arizona as an example of a society in which "the child is from infancy continuously conditioned to responsible social participation, while at the same time the tasks that are expected of it are adapted to its capacity. The contrast with our society is very great." Here the child makes no contribution until he can compete on an adult level. He is praised by adults when the spirit moves them, regardless of the standard of achievement he attains. Therefore, he is given no clear-cut standard for measuring himself.[37]

Instead of opportunities for serious accomplishment in our culture, we supply our children with expensive toys, hoping that these will occupy them and keep them from disturbing us. In actuality, even in today's world of the "educational toy," most of the toys adults give to children do not meet their needs for growth and involvement with the real world. Consequently, they are a source of frustration to the child, and he does not remain occupied with them for long.

The toy has become so important that people think it an aid to the intelligence; it is certainly better than nothing, but it is significant that the child quickly tires of a toy and wants new ones.[38]

Toys in fact seem to present a useless environment which cannot lead to any concentration of the spirit and which has no purpose; they are for minds astray in illusion. . . . And yet toys are the only things the adult has made for the child as an intelligent being.[39]

Why do we give the child toys that occupy him instead of involving him in the life around him in a meaningful way as they do in other cultures? Montessori felt it was because the adult in our culture realizes this would entail certain accommodations on his part, and he is so intent on his own production and achievement that he is unwilling to make them. The adult

sees that he must make an immense renunciation . . . surrender his environment, and this is incompatible with social life as it exists. In an adult environment the child is undoubtedly an extra-social being. But simply to shut him out, as has been done up till now, means a repression of his growth.[40]

Instead of giving the child toys that have no meaning for him, the adult must prepare special activities within his environment that will aid the child's development.

The solution of this conflict lies in preparing an environment adapted to these higher manifestations on the part of the child. When he says his first word there is no need to prepare anything and his baby language is heard in the house as a welcome sound. But the work of his small hands demands "motives of activity" in the form of suitable objects.[41]

How is the parent to go about preparing these activities? A clue can be taken from the discarded toys. Why does the child reject them? Because, according to Montessori, they do not bring the child into contact with reality.[42] What the child wants and needs are objects and activities that can serve as a preparation for the adult world where he realizes he is one day to take his place. When this is done, his response shows the parent he is on the right track.

> He does not care for things that are not in his usual environment because his work is to suit himself to his own adult world. [When] things are made for him in proportion to his size, and he can be active with them just as adults are active, his whole character seems to change and he becomes calm and contented.[43]
>
> One test of the correctness of educational procedure is the happiness of the child itself.[44]

The parent must observe his child closely, and watch for the kinds of activities he chooses spontaneously in his environment. The parent can then make them more available to the child by organizing them on the child's own level, and later by creating expansions and variations of them. The simpler he can make these activities, the better they will fit the child's needs. It is important to remember, too, that the child must be taught indirectly; verbal instructions are not helpful and may hinder the young child by distracting him: "However much you speak and speak and speak, you accomplish nothing because the child cannot take directly but only indirectly." [45] The principles outlined in describing the Montessori materials and the Fundamental Lesson in Chapter 2 are good guides to follow in setting up these activities. The parent can also include the child in his own activities as much as possible. Even a child of eighteen months can put spoons in the dishwasher or drawer, arrange cupboards, dust furniture, "fold" dishcloths, help to feed animals, dig in a garden. When desk work is necessary, a child of this age can work at his own table, making marks on paper with a pencil, folding papers, talking on a realistic model telephone. Trips outside the home can be arranged at a child's level and pace.

Parents whose children will not have a nursery or preschool experience may want to structure some preliminary academic activities at home. A visit to a good kindergarten or Montessori class might give them some constructive ideas. The best book available on such activities with Montessori materials is *Dr. Montessori's Own Handbook*. A catalogue of Montessori materials is available from Montessori Leermiddelenhmuis, A. Nienhuis, Melkwegstraat 4–6, The Hague, The Netherlands.

However, a word of caution is in order: a parent who is planning to work with his child at home with definite learning objectives in mind should have a realistic understanding of his own nature and that of his child, of their relationship together, and of his motivation in pursuing these activities. Many American parents overpower their children with too much enthusiasm and overdirection. Others are tense, anxious parents who expect too much of their children and themselves. Instead of placing one more demand on them both, parents might best concentrate on relaxing with their children and enjoying them—perhaps taking unhurried walks in the woods with a camera, field glasses, or magnifying glass.[46]

The role Montessori believed freedom played in the child's development has been discussed in earlier parts of this book. However, I would like to add a word on freedom, directed specifically to parents. In our rapidly changing culture, there is pressure on parents to give their children more and more "freedom." Increasingly, it is only the mature and confident parent who gives his child the guidance, limits, and leadership that are necessary for the development of true freedom. Montessori wrote in 1948,

> The main problem is the problem of freedom; its significance and repercussions have to be clearly understood. The adult's idea that freedom consists in minimizing duties and obligations must be rejected. . . . The freedom that is given to the child is not liberation from parents and teachers; it is not freedom from the laws of Nature or of the state or of society, but the utmost freedom for self-development and self-realization compatible with service to society.[47]

5

The Montessori Approach
Applied to Writing
and Reading

ALTHOUGH Dr. Montessori wrote many books on her general philosophy and method, she did not write a textbook explaining exact procedures in detail for either the home or the classroom. Perhaps she was apprehensive that such an explicit statement might tend to render her ideas inflexible. Parents or teachers might memorize certain techniques and procedures, and mechanically reproduce them with children. Nothing would be further from Montessori's concept of education as a living process, determined not by teacher or parent but by the child's inner powers. Hoping to avoid the all-too-human tendency to freeze methods used in the classroom into a rigid form, Montessori decided her teachers must each write their own textbook based on their individual understanding of Montessori education. The manual each Montessori teacher develops during her training is her own personal guidebook to refer to, revise, and add to throughout her teaching career. Montessori undoubtedly hoped that such a procedure would help her teachers view their teaching lives as a continuing process, subject to growth and change. Secondly, by writing her own guidebook, the Montessori teacher is forced to think through her personal approach to the materials and the children on a deeper level than if she were merely handed someone else's answers. This policy of asking each teacher to state her own understanding of Montessori education is consistent with a philosophy and method of education that asks children to discover their own answers, instead of expecting to appropriate and substitute someone else's experiences for their own.

The lack of a textbook on the specific application of Montessori has, however, led to some confusion for both parents at home and teachers in the classroom. It is difficult to see, for example, how children five and six years of age simply begin to write, and then to read, merely by being exposed to an environment based on the principles of freedom and discipline and in which sandpaper letters, movable alphabets, and various games have been placed. Obviously, it doesn't just happen. A precise and detailed account of this phenomenon would involve more explanation than is appropriate here. However, a brief indication of how Montessori education works out in application in this one area may give a deeper understanding of Montessori philosophy and method in general.

In understanding Montessori education in any area, it is important to remember that the approach is always indirect—never the direct one of traditional education. Montessori's enormous respect for the mysterious powers that form the child from the moment of conception led her to fear any direct interference with their unfolding.

> We are here to offer to this life, which came into the world by itself, the means necessary for its development, and having done that we must await this development with respect.[1]

The indirect approach Montessori advocated for helping the child to discover written communication begins at his birth. Because written communication is visualized language—and, as such, an extension of the child's oral language—it is important that his environment be saturated with human sound from his earliest moments. He should not be kept apart from social life even as a tiny infant, but included in all the family does. He should be talked to and listened to with patience and interest. He should be given the names of all the things in his environment, not just "tree," but "oak tree," "maple tree," etc., for this is the period of the Absorbent Mind, when he learns these things naturally. Later, he will have to memorize them, which will be not only more difficult but not nearly so likely to stimulate a life-long interest in these things. Just as the family must surround the baby with language, so it is important to surround him with the written word. He should see people reading books in his home as well as being exposed to the signs and written communications of the outer world, for in this way he develops a natural awareness of another form of communication in his environment.

Because of Montessori's infinite trust in the child's powers to teach himself, she did not devise a method for "teaching reading." Nor did she think it wise to decide upon a particular time when children should begin to read. Because of this approach, Montessori children typically do not remember learning to read, nor does the teacher remember teaching any particular one. The environment is so designed that all activities feed naturally toward the development of the skills required for reading, and thus reading is experienced as part of the process of living. This is in contrast to the emphasis on force-feeding reading to children, as in the traditional method, by presenting them one day with a book (the same for every child) in which are words that must be pronounced (aloud so everyone can hear) and then questions asked ("What did Jane say?" "What color was the ball?") that must be answered (again, so everyone can hear).

It was not only Montessori's trust in the child's powers that led her to approach reading in this natural way, but also her concept of the child as an active rather than a receptive being. She considered it the job of education not to fill the child with the techniques of reading but to free him for self-expression and communication. The question then became one of how to present opportunities for these to him without getting caught up in mechanics, which would keep the child from taking off on his own. This concentration on meaningfulness *versus* the mechanics of the written word led to a reversal in the procedure of reading before writing. In writing the child expresses his own thoughts through symbols; in reading he must comprehend the thoughts of another. Writing is a known to him, for he is giving his own language to another. In reading, he must deal with an unknown—the thoughts of another. The latter is obviously a far more complicated procedure.

What then are the needs of the child for writing? He must be able to use a writing instrument, have developed a lightness of touch, be able to keep within limits or space available for writing, know the shape of movement he wants to make—i.e., letters and their sounds—and he must be able to trace that movement. In addition to mastery of these mechanical processes, he must know nonphonetic or "puzzle" words, phonograms, general word construction and word study (prefixes, suffixes, masculine and feminine forms), and punctuation. He must have developed an enriched vocabulary and the concept that things have names, an appreciation of the exactness of word meanings and definitions, and a realization that words can be grouped into classifications. He must understand that words have functions and that the relationship of words and their position in a sentence is important. He must know and appreciate sentence construction.

If all of this knowledge is not to become a mechanical process for the child, the teacher must convey some sense of the mystery of language to him. In order to do this, she must keep alive within her an awareness of language as the unique acquisition of man, distinguishing him from the animals and the power through which he conquers the limitations of time, experiences all human emotion and historical knowledge, and leaves a legacy for future generations. The teacher must also convey to the child some concept of language as an agreement among peoples—an agreement that can be explored. In addition, people in different countries have made different agreements, and these, too, can be explored. The task for the teacher becomes one of preparing the child for a great exploration leading to communication between self and others, both living and dead, in this country and in others—a far different endeavor than merely teaching a child to write and read.

The preparation in the classroom for this exploration begins with the Daily Living exercises. Through these the child develops the control of movement and eye-hand coordination which will aid him in writing. The pouring of rice and later water from one small pitcher to another, the lacing and buttoning frames, silver polishing, the cutting of vegetables, the carrying of trays of equipment—all involve precise movements of the hand and body leading to coordination of sight and muscle control. These exercises also develop an understanding of the process and order involved in a complete cycle of activity with a beginning, middle, and end. In addition, as the first absorption with a precise activity, they begin the child's development of concentration and inner discipline. The integration of self and understanding of process that result from these exercises are important for any serious task the child will undertake.

The Sensorial Materials further expand the child's preparation by building on the order established in the child through the Daily Living exercises. The Pink Tower, the Geometric Cabinet, the Solid Cylinders, the Sound Cylinders, the Metal Insets, the many matching games, the Color Tablets, the Bells, to name only a few, develop his perceptual abilities, visual and auditory discrimination, and ability to compare and classify, all powers necessary for written language. In addition, his muscular control is being further refined in preparation for writing movements and holding a pencil. The tiny knobs used to lift the pieces of the Solid Cylinders, the Metal Insets, the puzzle maps, the Geometric Cabinet forms, etc., involve the pincer movement of the thumb and index fingers. The tactile exercises develop a lightness of touch and, in the case of the Touch Boards (boards of alternating strips of sandpaper and smooth wood), movement from left to right. The tracing of forms such as the Geometric Cabinet shapes (feeling around a wooden circle inset, etc.) trains the eye for exactness of shape and the muscles of hand and finger to follow the outline of a form in preparation for forming letters.

Language development runs parallel with these other activities. The children are read to often, from a wide variety of books about the lives of other people, other places, the life about them, and particularly the world of nature. The emphasis at this age is on widening the child's horizon in the real world. He is in the sensitive period for facts and he hungers for real knowledge. He is at this stage quite a literal person. When he says, "What is that?" or "Why is that?" he wants the adult to tell him what an object *really* is, or what is the *real* explanation he seeks. Sometime after the age of six, the child can share the adult's delight in fanciful answers because he, too, is in on the secrets of the real ones. It is then that books of fantasy, myth, and fairy tales are introduced.

Language development is also encouraged in the Montessori class through its total freedom of conversation. Through this freedom language becomes an integral part of the life of the classroom, and there is a continuous encouragement of self-expression and communication, child to child and child to adult. It is not necessary, therefore, to set aside artificial periods for communication, such as the "show and tell" times of traditional classrooms (*see* Appendix).

Vocabulary is enriched in a Montessori classroom in a number of unique ways. Precise names are used for all the objects in the environment, and there are a good many! All sorts of games are played, in addition to the usage of vocabulary in the natural use of material. ("Can you bring me the flag of Australia, the solid triangle, the color tablet?" "I did the hexagon today.") There are also many picture-card matching games that enrich vocabulary: cards of musicians, artists, paintings, tools, furnishings, foodstuffs; cards showing historical styles of clothing, housing, transportation; classifications of animals, reptiles, plant life, geometric shapes and forms, etc. These must all be made by the teacher. The more she manages to place in the environment, the more the children want. The child absorbs the vocabulary that goes with these cards because he is still in his sensitive period for language. If he does not encounter these names until later, he will have to "learn" them—a process that will have far less appeal for him. The materials, too, encourage the concept of classification by their orderly arrangement and division into categories of sensorial activities, Daily Living exercises, arithmetic, science, geography, etc.

Development of the large muscles, whose importance as a foundation for mental activities is just now receiving wide attention, is encouraged in Montessori through the design of the classroom activities. For example, each red rod is carried separately, involving ten different trips between rug and shelf, and again ten separate trips to return the rods. The rods themselves are held on the ends, partly so the child feels the difference between short and long, and shorter, shortest, etc., but also because it is one meter from the beginning to the end of the longest rod, a healthy stretch for a three-year-old. Because the child is in his sensitive period for motor development, he gets a particular satisfaction out of the carrying and stretching required for using the materials. As the child grows older and his motor development becomes established, he does not have this same interest in large-muscle movement. Therefore, the equipment he uses becomes smaller in scale and does not entail so many trips to the shelves. Montessori devised two other activities to aid the child in his motor development: the Walking on the Line exercise and the Silence Game. Walking on the Line and its variations help the child to develop his sense of balance (carrying a glass of water on a tray), control of movement (run faster; walk as slowly as you can), and an awareness of his right and left side (carry a flag in your right hand). The Silence Game develops control of movement and an awareness of self in relation to space and to others. It also brings an awareness of sound to the child, and stimulates his powers of observation of his environment. Perhaps because it encourages an inner quiet and searching of self, it seems to promote the child's creative powers as well.

After all four of these areas—the Daily Living exercises, the Sensorial Materials, Language Development, and Motor Development—have been contributing for a number of months to the child's preparation for the exploration of language, the teacher begins to introduce activities more directly related to written language. She begins by giving the child an opportunity to explore sounds on a more conscious basis than he would have encountered randomly in his environment. The teacher's aim is to help him establish an awareness of specific sounds in preparation for an introduction of the symbol for that sound. The teacher may make the sound "mmmm," then pronounce words with this sound—*m*other, some*d*ay, dru*m*—and invite the child to think of some, too. This is done casually in off-moments, but one day, when the teacher is certain the child is aware of the sound "mmmm," she might say, "Do you know you can *see* 'mmmm,' in fact you can *feel* it!" It is then she introduces the first sandpaper letter to the child. This is done individually in order to gain the maximum opportunity to dramatize for the child the power and mystery of this symbol that will lead to written communication.

The sandpaper letters are letters cut out in sandpaper and mounted on smooth boards approximately six inches high. The vowels are mounted on red boards, the consonants on

blue ones. Later the distinction between vowels and consonants will be built on this earlier visual foundation. Only
the sound of the letter is given to the child. (The name of a
letter is of no use to a three-year-old, although this is the
first information he is given about letters in American culture.) The sandpaper serves to control the child's movements
when he feels the letter, for he knows by touch when he
has slipped off the letter onto the smooth board. Control of
error concerning the letter's direction and place also results
from the letters' being pasted on the oblong tablets, for the
child can see when he has placed the letter sideways or up-
side down. The letters are in cursive writing because the
movement of the hand over them can be more flowing, as op-
posed to the abrupt movements required for printed letters.
This gives the child a more natural movement for writing,
the activity that will precede reading. In addition, there is a
more natural linking together of hand and mind in the forming of cursive letters, and, therefore, they are more easily
imprinted in the child's memory. The children make a very
natural transition from cursive to printed letters about the
time they begin to read, which may be anywhere from five
to seven, or for some children even later. One letter is placed
upon each tablet in order to isolate it from among all others.
This principle of isolation of new knowledge, running through
Montessori education, helps the child to focus on a new
discovery. Therefore, there are no friezes of letters or alphabet about the room at this stage.

The teacher first traces the letter *m* with the first and
second fingers of the dominant hand, simultaneously pronouncing the sound "mmm." This is a very slow and deliberate movement. If this is a purely mechanical action, the
child may or may not become interested. The teacher must
try, therefore, to recapture some of her own feeling for these
keys to language in order that the child may recognize their
potential. The teacher invites the child to trace the letter and
pronounce the sound "mmm." ("You can touch it, too. Now

you know what 'mmm' looks like. There are other letters, too!" Always, the teacher works from what is known to the child to the unknown, and leaves a deposit on which to build the next discovery.) By tracing the letter with the index finger of his dominant hand, the child builds a muscular memory of the shape of the letter he will one day write. If he has a tendency to press too hard, he is told to move his fingers lightly over the letter so that it tickles, thus encouraging the lightness of touch needed for writing. Various games, such as tracing the letters in the air or tracing them blindfolded, help the child consolidate which way the letters go. The child is not encouraged to write the letters learned on paper or to read words from them at this point. This exercise with the sandpaper letters is an exploration in the sound of language and the shape of the symbol for this sound; it is not an exercise in writing. Because some educators have attempted to reach older children through the sandpaper letters, it should be mentioned that they are designed for use during the child's sensitive period for touch and sound. This means they are of little use much beyond the age of four. If letters and their sounds are to be introduced at a later age, other tools, based on the child's sensitive periods at that age, must be devised for presenting them.

After eight or ten letters have been used in this way, and the sound and the symbol firmly connected in the mind by means of Séguin's three-period lesson (always used in Montessori to establish that learning has taken place), the Movable Alphabet is introduced. This is a box divided into individual compartments containing cardboard letters of the alphabet, again with the consonants in blue, the vowels in red. The Movable Alphabet enables the child to put together symbol and sound in order to render his own language visible. The teacher sounds out a three-letter phonetic word such as "cat," picking each letter as she makes the sound, and placing them together in left-to-right progression on a mat. This material is not used to encourage reading or writing—only the me-

chanical production of the child's words and later his phrases
and sentences as well. To put together the symbols mentally,
as is required in reading, is too difficult a task at this stage;
nor is the child asked to write with paper and pencil. Parents
are educated to understand that the child must not be expected to bring work home at this age, for the work of the
young child is interior.

As the child begins spontaneously to compose small stories
with the Movable Alphabet, he will need words he cannot
sound out phonetically. The teacher gives him the word he
wants matter-of-factly, with no attempt to teach him the in-
tricacies of English spelling. Nor is any attempt made to
correct words that are not properly spelled, but which he is
satisfied with. The idea here is only to encourage the child
to express his own thoughts.

Simultaneously with the introduction of the sandpaper
letters and the Movable Alphabet, another piece of equipment
is presented. The Metal Insets, designed to contribute to the
development of the mechanical writing skills, are red metal
frames with blue insets, both of geometric shapes: circle,
triangle, trapezium, pentagon, quatrefoil, etc. The child takes
the frame and inset he wishes to use, a piece of square
paper the size of the frame, and three colored pencils. He
traces the frame with one colored pencil, making the geometric form of the frame. He then puts the inset on this
newly drawn form, and taking another pencil draws around
the inset. The form is now outlined in two separate colors.
Now lines are drawn up and down and side to side, until
the form is completely covered with the third color. Later, the
child uses several insets together, superimposing different geometric figures one upon another and creating original designs.
The purpose of the insets is primarily to develop the muscular
control needed to wield a pencil, to stay within an outline,
and to move lightly across the paper in a controlled movement. The Metal Insets complete the possibility for an explosion into writing, for the child now knows letters, can

compose words and sentences, and has the necessary control of his hand movements.

There is a fourth area developed throughout this period that will make this explosion more meaningful to the child when it does occur: the area of vocabulary enrichment of written words. Matching picture cards of all the areas explored earlier on a sensorial level are now labeled. On one set of cards the labels are printed beneath the pictures. The other set has no printed labels, but unattached plain ones are in the same box. The teacher takes a set of these and writes the label for each matching picture while the child watches. After this introduction the child can match his own labels, using the already labeled cards to check his work. The teacher always writes the labels for the child during the first presentation. This helps to fix the word in the child's mind, in addition to exposing him to the proper forming of the letters and presenting the possibility of writing itself. Labels are also made for all the objects in the environment. All of these vocabulary materials are made by the teacher, and her ingenuity and conscientiousness in producing a wealth of them will largely determine the child's continued interest in written words at this stage.

There will come a time when the child does not want to put away his story, as he must, when he has formed it by means of the Movable Letters. This is the natural motivation that produces the transition from the Movable Alphabet to writing. It comes from the child's own desires, then, and not the desires of teacher or parent. This self-propulsion of the child toward the development of writing must not be interfered with by either the anxieties or the praises of adults. When the child has been exposed to the proper environment, writing develops as naturally as oral language did in an earlier period. It should be treated just as matter-of-factly.

About this same time, which may be approximately six months after the introduction of the Movable Alphabet, the child realizes he can not only make "c-a-t," making each sound separately, but that he can make "cat," a word of synthesized sound which can be experienced as a whole. Up to this time the child working with the Movable Alphabet has asked the teacher, "Did I make 'pig'?" Now he says, "Come and see! I made 'pig'!" This is obviously a moment of great excitement for the child. He has literally "discovered reading." This is an excellent example of the Montessori apparatus bringing an already acquired skill of the child to consciousness. He had the power to synthesize the word before he knew he could do it. "I didn't know I knew that!" is a phrase often heard in Montessori classrooms. Thus the child develops a sense of wonder at his own powers, and this wonder becomes a motivating force toward further acquisitions.

Occasionally, it happens that the child needs a little help in making this transition to seeing the words he has made as a whole. In this case, the teacher forms a word with the Movable Alphabet and says, "I wonder if you can find one of these for me?" or "Can you tell me about this?" She is careful not to say, "I wonder if you can *read* this?" If the child is ready, this request usually gives him the lead that will carry him into synthesization.

The Montessori child, then, does not learn to read from books, but through a long process of indirect preparation. When he takes a book to read, he already knows how. This is very important for the child's initial response to books. Who wants to read "See, Jane, see. Come and see. See me."? A child's first encounter with books he is going to read himself must involve those he will find worth exploring. This can only be accomplished if the reading of books themselves is saved for the final act of the drama.

When the teacher is aware that a child reads back the words he has made on his mat with the Movable Alphabet, she introduces him to the Phonetic Object Game. This game initially involves a small box of three-letter phonetic objects such as pin, cat, cup, etc. The teacher writes the word "pin" on a small piece of paper, and says, "Can you give me what I want?" (Again, she does not say, "Can you *read* this?") The label and object are then matched together, pronouncing each label with the placing action. After all the labels are made, the child can use the game alone. A tremendous quantity of these object games must be organized by the teacher, for the more knowledge that is made available to the child, the more he is stimulated to explore language.

After the Phonetic Object Game is presented, two new ideas are introduced, phonograms and "puzzle words." Phonograms are introduced through the Object Game. The usual phonetic objects are introduced, but the last object in the box contains a phonogram such as in "ship." Only one unphonetic object is introduced, again preserving the principle of isolation of new knowledge. The teacher explains, "Sometimes when letters sit together they make a different sound. They're partners, and they produce something new to each of them." She then writes *sh* on the label in one color and *ip* in another. Two boxes of smaller Movable Alphabets are now introduced, one yellow, one green. The teacher begins the phonogram *sh* and says, "Can you think of more words with *sh*?" They explore the alphabet, using the vowels and consonants to make new words with the *sh* sound, including those with *sh* in the middle or end of the word (fishing, fish, etc.). The dictionary can be used to see if indeed a real word has been made in this exploration. Phonogram cards and booklets are also prepared which the child can use on his own or with others. Additional difficulties are introduced through the Object Game or the Puzzle Word games. Cards of "puzzle words," such as boat, coat, float are gathered together in envelopes bearing a label of the family to be introduced, such as *oa*, *ai*, etc., and again picture cards and labels are the devices used for the identification. Other envelopes contain words such as knife, cough, laugh, jump, etc. The teacher makes no attempt to explain the causes for these irregularities at this age. The sensitive period for the source of words occurs sometime during the junior level from six to nine, and it is then that the roots of words are explored.

Classified picture cards are introduced at this point (all reptiles, all mammals, all geometric shapes, etc.; and later, parts of reptiles, parts of mammals, etc.). Definition cards are also presented: a definition such as "an island is a body of land surrounded by water" is matched with a picture of an island. The child has had familiarity with these definitions previously on a concrete level. For example, the concepts of an island, an isthmus, a peninsula, etc., have been introduced sensorially a year or more earlier through the geography material. Trays were prepared with clay representing the land shape to be identified. The child poured water into the tray, thus forming his own island, etc. Next he experienced an island in the abstract through drawings in one of the matching picture-card games. Finally, he has met the definition itself through the Definition Card Game.

The children are now somewhere between five and seven, and have been in a Montessori class for three or four years. This means some are in the six-to-nine or junior Montessori level, and equivalent to the first graders of a traditional school. Throughout this time there has always been a special place in the room for reading—a comfortable and attractive spot with rugs on the floor, rocking chairs, and a large supply of good books. All the children look at the books from time to time, and those who are familiar with words read them whenever they choose. It is a common sight to see one of the older children reading aloud to one or more three-year-olds.

An exploration of the functions of words is now begun with those children who are ready, and this is the first time the phrase "introduction to reading" is used in Montessori. All that has gone before has simply been a foundation for this introduction. The exploration is carried out by means of equipment through which the function of words is exhibited.

One such piece of equipment used traditionally in Montessori schools is a complete model farm with all of its component parts. A model city, factory, shop, or school could be used, but it must be a model that presents the opportunity to show words representing a great many qualities. Small labels are made for each object in the model. The child is accustomed to words that name things. Now the concept of *the* horse, meaning the only one, or *a* horse, meaning one of many, is presented. Next the idea of describing words is presented. The teacher may say, "Give me the horse. Oh, I didn't mean that one. I want the *white* horse." She writes "white," and puts it between the labels "the" and "horse." (The words "adjective," "noun," and "article" are not introduced at this point. The intent is only to give the key that different words do different things; to add any more information would introduce a useless complication.) Symbols are used to represent the word functions presented: a black triangle is placed over the noun, a small blue triangle over the modifying word or adjective. Later, a red circle will denote a verb, a smaller orange circle the adverb, and so on for all the parts of speech. The child pastes these symbols above the words in phrases or sentences he makes. These symbols are used for several reasons. Because the child is still in the sensitive period for movement, the hand must be involved as well as the eye if the child's interest is to be maintained. In addition, the sensorial experience of the symbols helps to fix the functions of the words in the child's mind. Later, replacing the black triangle with the word "noun" will involve a simple substitution based on a well-established concept.

The position of the word in a phrase is also emphasized at the time of the introduction of word function. The teacher may place "white" and "the horse," saying, "Does that sound right? I guess we'd better put it here. 'The white horse.' That's better." This exploration of word position goes on throughout the learning of word function. The child discovers that sometimes the sense remains, and sometimes it doesn't.

A great many more games are introduced to explore the functions of words: Object Boxes to teach singular and plural forms; a Detective Game played with labels for the materials in the room ("Find the smallest pink cube, the small blue scalene right-angled triangle"); the Command Game (the child reads *silently* slips of paper on which commands are printed, and carries out the action) and Command Games introducing transitive and intransitive verbs (run—a command involving no direct object; drink a glass of water—a command involving a direct object).

All during this further exploration of word function, the child has been reading on his own. This is possible for him because the isolation of difficulties in the earlier preparation has meant that, when reading came to him, it came in a full form. In Montessori education this full form is referred to as "total reading." Continued exercises serve to give forceful impressions that lead the child to notice the importance of each item in a sentence—not only the meaning of each word, but its position in the phrase or sentence. It is the child's continuing experience with reading that gives him the foundation and interest in these grammar exercises. In this case, it is the reading that serves as an indirect preparation for the exercises, and not the other way around, as previously.

By now the child has moved on to the junior level of Montessori and he is ready for the nomenclature of grammar. The names "noun," "article," etc., are introduced through a wooden box divided into compartments, one marked "article," the other "noun." The child places the word "the" in the "article" compartment, "car" in the "noun" compartment. Other boxes include the adjective, verb, adverb, etc., introducing all the parts of speech one at a time. Sentence analysis is begun with the object of helping the child to develop his power to convey exactly what he wishes in his writing. This analysis is carried out initially by means of cutting sentences into words and placing the subject on a black disc with a black wooden arrow on which the words "What is it? Who is it?" are printed, pointing toward it. Next comes a red disc which the verb is placed upon; and next to it is another black arrow saying, "Who? What?" pointing toward a black disc on which the direct object is to be placed. This sentence analysis continues, gradually introducing increasingly complicated sentences (i.e., those with clauses of source, of time, purpose, or manner, attributive clauses, etc.). This analysis lays a good foundation for sentence diagramming and composition, and for the exploration of writing styles of various authors.

Because he has been exposed to so much information in the Montessori environment, the child is now in a position to produce a wealth of compositions on many different subjects: history, nature, geography, music, etc. It is the very careful past preparation through the Montessori environment that has made possible a tremendous flowering of creative writing at this young age. This writing, and the advanced level of reading it leads into, appears as a natural expansion of the child's powers in a Montessori classroom. This expansion occurs in all other areas of knowledge as well, and in each case the procedure is the same. The needs of the child in his sensitive periods are matched with an indirect preparation to meet those needs. It is this that makes it possible for the Montessori child to build one foundation out of another in an ever-extending reach for self-construction.

6

Why Montessori Today

MONTESSORI HAS already made a great contribution to education in Europe and Asia, but it is to America in the 1970's that her work has particular pertinence. The revolution that technological and biological breakthroughs have wrought has resulted in unprecedented changes in human life-styles. Affluence and luxuries for a large portion of the population, instant communication through electronic media via worldwide satellites, the preservation and prolongation of human life, the possibilities now being explored of artificially reproducing and modifying that life, the overpopulating and polluting of the earth, and the ever-present threat of its total destruction by man himself—all these present problems that call for an entirely different response to life than man has ever given before. It becomes increasingly obvious that traditional education, based as it is upon handing to the student the answers of another era, is no longer sufficient. If young people are to meet the challenge of survival that faces them today, it is imperative that their education develop to the fullest extent possible their potential for creativity, initiative, independence, inner discipline, and self-confidence. This is the central focus of Montessori education.

In addition to this generalized aim, there are several areas where the Montessori approach can make specific contributions to our culture. One of these is the Montessori attitude toward work. The very core of the Montessori philosophy and method is its approach to the work of both the child and the adult. By "work" Montessori did not mean mechanical drudgery, but physical and mental activity freely chosen by an individual—activity that has meaning for him because it promotes his own growth or contributes to society. Montessori believed this activity was natural to the child and the most important single influence on his development. "Are we going to free the child from work? Such attempt will be like uprooting a plant or taking a fish out of water." [1] We do not take seriously the young child's instinct for work in our culture. Instead, we encourage him to play all day. Even if a young child goes to pre-school, it is assumed he will not be directly motivated toward intellectual development and that he will have to be led to it without his being aware of what is happening. Compare Montessori's attitude toward work for the young child with the one implicit in the following statement from a brochure for pre-school Head Start classes in a large Midwestern city. It is not atypical.

To a four year old, pre-school classes are fun—

Playing with dolls in the playhouse corner. Building with blocks and joyfully watching them tumble down around you with noisy crashes that make the teacher jump.

Games outside with balls and jumpropes. Walks. Quiet times listening to soft music. Story time with books and pictures and flannel boards. Marching in the rhythm band.

Chatting with classmates, talking to the teacher, learning, sharing, caring.

A fun-filled morning or afternoon gone and each child has experienced something new.

Without his knowing it, his teacher and her aide have subtly guided him in language development, perceptual skills, motor control, creative activities, and social behavior. . . .

Pre-school may look like fun through the eyes of a four-year-old but it's really a very special learning experience. [Italics mine.]

Recently there have been signs of a shift away from the

overemphasis on play for the very young. This is due in part to recent research on the cognitive development of infants. Studies done by Jerome Bruner of the Institute of Cognitive Studies at Harvard University, Jean Piaget of the Institute of Educational Science at the University of Geneva, and others have presented new evidence of the great learning abilities of infants. Man, being what he is, may use this new knowledge to further the fulfillment and happiness of the child by providing him with better environments to suit the child's needs, or he may use this information to demand more of what the adult wants from the child at an ever earlier age.

The hoop of adult requirements for the baby can go up and up, and the infant taught to jump ever higher through it, just as has happened with older children. The danger of such exploitation is very real in our society today, where a reaction against some of the unwise excesses permitted to the child is threatening to gain momentum. This could lead to even greater dangers for the young child's life than the earlier belief that all the young child wanted, or really should be doing, was to play all day. If this misdirected emphasis on work occurs, Montessori philosophy can serve as a balancing influence. It takes into account the child's instinct and legitimate need for purposeful activity, but, because this activity is constructed on the basis of the child's own desires and needs, it does not permit the exploiting of the child's talents by the adult.

Montessori is also pertinent to our times for the adult world in regard to work. Traditionally, educators in America have not acted upon nor understood the nature of the young child's instinct for work. Our culture did, however, in the past have some concept of the meaningfulness of work in the adult's life. In recent years, the emphasis on this meaningfulness has shifted and deteriorated. Work is viewed as important primarily in the search for status, money, and consumer goods —relative satisfactions which are subject to constant disruption through exposure to those who have more or to advertising stimulation to seek more for ourselves. As a result, never in the history of man has a whole nation been so in need of a renewed appreciation of the meaning of work. Montessori education, with its understanding of the generative and regenerative force in human life, is uniquely suited to help meet this need.

Because our society has endangered the life of a whole planet, and perhaps the universe itself, by our disrespect for the laws of nature, Montessori's approach to nature has special significance for our culture. Montessori regarded man's interdependence with nature as both physical and spiritual.

> But if for the physical life it is necessary to have the child exposed to the vivifying forces of nature, it is also necessary for his psychical life to place the soul of the child in contact with creation.[2]

In today's world children do not have this needed relationship with nature.

> In our time and in the civilized environment of our society children, however, live very far distant from nature, and have few opportunities of entering into intimate contact with it or of having direct experience with it. . . . We have all made ourselves prisoners voluntarily, and have finished up by loving our prison and transferring our children to it. Nature has, little by little, been restricted in our conception to the growing of flowers, and to the domestic animals which we depend on for food.[3]

It is not hard to understand that the child reared in such estrangement from his natural life should grow into an adult who plunders, pollutes, and destroys nature without even being conscious of what he is doing. Botany, zoology, and the study of land forms are an integral part of the Montessori curriculum, and many a six-year-old Montessori child knows more about the classification of plants and the care of living things than the average adult. Thus, the Montessori child is well prepared to become an ecologically responsible adult.

Montessori brought nature into the classroom, but, even more important, she believed in the child living in nature.

The idea, however, of *living* in nature is the most recent acquisition to education. Indeed the child needs to live naturally, and not only to know nature. The most important fact really is the liberation of the child . . . from the bonds which isolate him in the artificial life created by living in cities.[4]

A modern program in keeping with Montessori's belief is the Outward Bound program. This program for both boys and girls, sixteen-and-one-half years and older, from all walks of life, is a unique twenty-six-day experience in some of the remotest wilderness areas of our country. A participant lives with nature in its rawest form, usually with a group of nine to twelve others, but for at least three days he lives totally alone—and in so doing comes to a better understanding of nature, his fellow human beings, and himself.[5] A combination of a Montessori School and an Outward Bound program would be a fascinating experiment in contemporary education.

Another area in which the Montessori approach is particularly meaningful today concerns family life. Montessori emphasized the family as the natural unit for the nurture and protection of the child, and stressed particularly the uniqueness of the mother's relationship to the child, beginning at birth. In our society, where family life is being rapidly diminished and undermined, this support of the family is much needed. Montessori's inclusion of the parents in the life of the classroom and the guidance they are given in carrying out their role at home appears to be especially meaningful (*see* Appendix). Her concept, too, of the family as an extended unit is a valid point at a time when grandparents, aunts, uncles, and cousins are seldom part of the family's daily life.

Montessori's emphasis on childhood as the other dimension of human life is another important principle for today. Our society, bent as it is on a breakneck pace of production and achievement at all costs, desperately needs to work toward the balance that seeing the world through the eyes of the child gives. The child, like all living things, has his own natural laws. Recognizing them and adjusting our pace and tempo to them are beneficial to the adult, who has lost much of his own natural rhythm of being. Respect for a child's needs may help us in rediscovering our own and may in turn make us more tolerant of the needs of the elderly. Thus, the whole cycle of human life gains in dignity and understanding. If our eyes were more consistently on the child, as Montessori counseled, we simply could not do the kinds of inhuman things we do to children, to nature, to others, to ourselves.

In the emphasis on the development of human potential, work, man's interdependence with nature, the importance of family, and the meaning of the child to adult life, Montessori is significant for rich and poor alike. It is, however, its application to educational problems in the inner city where Montessori may first receive wide recognition in the United States today. Montessori is the only widely publicized, worldwide educational method that has had great success with the poor. The Case dei Bambini where Montessori made her first seminal discoveries in the education of young children were, in fact, day-care centers serving the most oppressed area in all of Rome, the San Lorenzo quarter.

One of the major reasons for Montessori's success with the children of the poor may be its lack of assumption of prelearned skills. Because Montessori began her work first with retarded children and then with children from the most deprived of backgrounds, she could not take any previous knowledge for granted. She built into her method the simplest of life's experiences—how to wash, dress, move about, carry things; how to hear, touch, and see. Every skill had to be presented from its most primitive beginnings: muscles were developed for holding a pencil before the pencil was given, an object was handled before a name was given. A careful path was always laid from the undeveloped to the developed, from the concrete to the abstract. This is, of course, important for all children, who begin their learning as infants with undeveloped brains. But with these children, where many steps usually taken for granted have been missed in earlier years, it can make the difference between the success and failure of a human life.

Montessori's emphasis on the development of positive self-image through work and real accomplishment has special meaning for the poor. Surrounded as he is likely to be by despair and defeat, there is almost no way for the inner-city child to develop trust in life or in his own powers. By achieving success on his own with the materials in the classroom, the child begins to understand his own value and talent. Highly important here is the Montessori emphasis on independence in learning, for if the inner-city child is to succeed in life, he will most likely have to do it without the kinds of support the middle-class child may receive. Because research shows that the teacher's image of the child is vital to his growth, the Montessori teacher's belief in the child's ability to develop through the materials should also be stressed. Perhaps because Montessori began by doing the "impossible" with children, this spirit of faith in the child has continued to pervade Montessori education to a unique degree.

Further, the beauty and structure of the Montessori environment has special significance to the inner-city child who may live with disorder and ugliness in his physical world. More than others, he may need beauty to awaken his love and interest in his environment, and order and structure through which to find purpose and meaning in life.

Probably most meaningful of all, the relationship Montessori develops with the parent has special significance for the poor. Because the environment of the home and the attitude and aspirations of the parent have more impact on the child than any other single influence, the parent's growth is at least as important for the child as his school experience. Montessori regarded the parent as a partner in the child's schooling. This recognition of the parent's legitimate role in the child's education can give the parent a new way of viewing himself and the school. The school is no longer seen as the authority issuing orders to parent and child alike. Instead, the parent is invited into the classroom. He shares in what is going on there and in the hopes for the future of the child and the class. The teacher demonstrates to him the materials his child uses to learn, and he is then free to try them himself. The step-by-step procedure leading from simple to complex, concrete to abstract, makes sense to him, and he can follow it through from beginning to end much as his child does. The order and simple beauty of the classroom are readily apparent, and the way they serve the child explained. The parent becomes aware of the teacher's respect for his child's work and her confidence in him. There is no discussion of the need for grades or rewards, nor of the physical punishment used *consistently* in the finest modern inner-city schools of today. (At a recent teachers' meeting in such a school, there was a lengthy discussion and an actual vote taken on whether it was better to use two rulers strapped together or a paddle for punishment. You have to know personally the very enlightened and concerned principals and teachers who are using these methods to be sufficiently shocked and disappointed.)

As we have seen, Montessori advocated frequent meetings with parents. These meetings are particularly important where a middle-class teacher teaches in an inner-city school, for they enable her to know the parent as a person with his own culture and concerns. These meetings are not structured like the potentially threatening twice-yearly interview of many inner-city schools. They are designed to be relaxed and informal, and include the teacher's coming to the child's home and taking part in activities with the child and parent after school. In this way, the teacher gets to know the family as a whole, and the parent has an opportunity to seek her help with the raising of the other children. Here the Montessori teacher can have a particularly beneficial influence. Parents of inner-city children often tend to punish their young children for accidents or exploratory behavior with a severity not usually seen in middle-class homes. They train their children for passivity, unaware they are preventing the growth of their intelligence. Through his experience in the classroom and inter-action with the teacher, the parent may become more aware and more tolerant of the young child's need to explore his world and to try to do things for himself.

Because Montessori is especially designed to operate with assistants to the teacher, parents are often brought into the classroom on a professional basis. When this happens, it should be emphasized that the parent is not treated as aides are in many traditional settings, where they act more in the capacity of diversion or keepers of discipline. In a Montessori setting the teacher tries to give the parent-assistant an understanding of the method and materials so that he can be a true partici-pant in the learning process. Again, it should be emphasized, this is possible in Montessori to a unique degree because assistants have been an integral part of the method since its inception. Traditionally, they have been trained in whole or in part by the teacher herself, and no previous knowledge or background in education is necessary. This use of assistants is not limited to parents, of course, and is a helpful source of employment to other men and women in the ghetto com-munity as well.

The poor themselves have responded with enthusiasm to Montessori education, which is the best evidence that it has special meaning for them. They attend the meetings with the teacher and seem to welcome the closer contact with her. They spread the word about Montessori in their community so that others begin to ask for it, too. When a Montessori classroom in one public school was going to close because of a cost-cutting program, it was the parents who took the initiative in keeping it going. In a Head Start Montessori class where the same situation occurred, the parents actually took over the responsibility for the class, and have kept it going with the help of a local church. What is there about Montessori education that these parents like? These are some of the answers parents of children in inner-city Montessori classes have given me.

From a mother who also teaches in a Montessori class:

"These children have so many fears—fear of punishment and fear they won't succeed. They won't try anything difficult. They're afraid of danger. They won't even go on the swings or slides. Little by little, in the Montessori classroom, you can see the relief coming."

(I thought of the public school classrooms in the area I had seen—the oppressive stillness, the inactivity, the furtive looks, the parroting of answers for teacher or visitor, the humiliation of failing in front of others, and always the threat of punishment for not following constant orders: sit up straight, don't talk to each other, read these pages, do this messy paper over. What does this do to a child who is more afraid than anything else?)

More mothers:

"These children need to be proud of themselves, and they need values—because they are black, especially because they are black."

"My child is black and he's bright. In the Montessori class they learn and they're active. Those children are reaching out. They didn't start out that way. Something happened to them there. It makes them want to reach out."

"They've got a chance to find themselves when they're young. They don't just teach reading, writing, and arithmetic the way most schools do. They can be anything they want, a poet, maybe. Nobody's forcing them. They use *all* their minds."

"The teacher comes to your house. She had three children to dinner, and then went back with one of them to their house. She knows all the other children in the family. Those are *her* children. Most teachers, the children are just *in their rooms.*"

"Those children have independence. They've got their own ideas, and you can't talk them out of it."

"They enjoy each other. It's like they're part of each other, instead of who they sit in back of, or next to. And they're kind to each other. The older ones help the younger ones. They're not competing."

"What I'm afraid of is what's going to happen to them in a regular class. Some won't adjust now, they just won't." *

"What I've seen is, the children around here in that class can read, they can *really* read. Instead of playing with Mickey Mouse toys, they're reading."

From fathers:

"They teach the individual child. It's not day care. They really learn something."

"They learn how to be independent, to maneuver on their own."

"They let a child feel its way. You can't tell how far they might get, the greatness they might achieve."

"They value the child. They build on his strengths. It's not just conform and adjust and be controlled."

"Most schools, you're nobody or you're not important. These children learn who they are, find out what they can do."

The following statement on Montessori was prepared by an unusually articulate young widowed mother with six children, several of whom have been in federally funded and public school Montessori classes for a number of years.

* This remark illustrates the awareness of even the inner-city parent of the wide differences in Montessori and traditional education. In reality, most Montessori children make the transition to more traditional schooling without much difficulty. This has been the experience in other parts of the world where Montessori schools have flourished for many years. In this country objective quantitative evidence is currently being collected by Dr. June Scirra and her research team at the University of Cincinnati (*see* Appendix).

If we have the Montessori method and early school and it was perfected to its most fullest, we would not have this school dropout problem that we have now. The money would not have to be spent bussing them and for special programs for these children. The money would be concentrated on getting the best Montessori teachers in it, maybe to send some of our present teachers back to school and give them the Montessori training, then use it and learn all we can about it and educate our children and to show them what a beautiful thing the process of learning can really be. . . . Montessori schools show—open up to you—it lays it all out openly for you—what's available for you. You have an opportunity to take what you want, to go in the direction which is fulfilling to you rather than have someone tell you you have to have so much this, so much that, so much that. Well, who in the world—I mean, really, being really realistic—who in the world knows what you need better than you do. If you are a well-adjusted person, which Montessori school I believe contributes to greatly is helping you to see yourself what you are, to accept yourself what you are, to respect yourself for your abilities and not to—sort of—down yourself and belittle yourself because you don't know as much as your neighbor do. . . . I believe that every child wants to know. I don't believe that any child likes to have an adult to keep telling him what something is. The child is curious, and when they are curious at this early age, I believe that their curiosity should be fed. . . . I don't think society is ready to accept the fact that our children are very intelligent and are being held back by society, and that's why I think it important that the inner-city child has the best education, which is the Montessori education, which does encourage a child to learn, to be curious, to be interested, to make learning a beautiful process. The old way, or method, has not worked. It is time for a change and it is time for a change now, or this vicious cycle of trying to repair damage of years ago will be repeated time and time again. . . . I see the Montessori child coming up from the age of three, completing high school, absorbing every bit of knowledge that is put before him, excelling in the subjects in the fields that interest him most. I see him as a peacemaker because he is able to solve his problems, he's able to think and to reason. He is not looking to the textbooks for answers but he is using his own inner self which is contained within himself. I believe that society is afraid of our children learning too much.

Montessori does have an important contribution to make to the American educational scene today—both for the middle-class child and the inner-city child. But is it possible to begin enough Montessori classes throughout the country, particularly in large city school systems, to influence the existing educational methods? There are two major areas to discuss in considering the practical aspects of applying Montessori practices to the mainstream of American education: the availability of teachers and the question of comparative costs with other educational systems.

In regard to teachers, there are two directions to follow: the training of new teachers or the retraining of experienced teachers. There are advantages and disadvantages to both approaches, and some combination of the two may be the most effective procedure to follow. New teachers who do not have to unlearn old behaviors may more readily accept and be able to carry out Montessori beliefs and practices. However, there may be problems both of supply and of replacing teachers who already have tenure. If experienced teachers are to be retrained, they will have to be convinced that Montessori education is a better approach to teaching than what they have known before. Already they feel underpaid, overworked, and unappreciated, and they are on strike across the country. This is not hard to understand. Teachers are discouraged because it is impossible for them to meet the demands being placed on them. They are asked to spend their days in the exhausting position of having to control and dominate children. They must herd, push, and pull them as one body through a set curriculum. Only those who have had to attempt this inhuman and unnatural endeavor could possibly appreciate the strain it places on the teacher who singlehandedly must accomplish it. The experienced teacher may well accept the opportunity to learn a new approach to teaching that would relieve her of this absurd burden. Experience so far has shown teachers who have been exposed to them *are* interested in the highly sophisticated techniques and materials for individualized learning Montessori provides, and in the Montessori practice of grouping children into larger age blocks (*see* Appendix).

In regard to the cost of Montessori education, there is a myth that operating expenses have to be higher for Montessori than other approaches to education. This myth has grown for several reasons: first because Montessori has existed mostly in pre-schools in this country. Montessori teachers for three–to–six-year-olds have as much training as many grade-school teachers, and work a full day whether the children are in the classroom for a whole day or not. Therefore they do receive higher salaries than nursery-school teachers, who have fewer requirements in terms of training and who traditionally work a half-day. However, Montessori teachers on the grade-school level receive the same salary as other public and private school teachers.

Secondly, there is the expense of an assistant in a Montessori classroom. In the three–to–six-year-old group, this is not an additional expense over traditional methods because most state requirements set a ratio of one adult to eight children in the lower age-levels of all classrooms. However, from kindergarten on, most traditional classrooms in the past have operated with no assistants. This situation has been changed in many inner-city schools today through the influx of federal funds for this purpose. Where no such funds are available, volunteer assistants—parents, siblings, or student-teachers— might assist in Montessori classrooms. Because Montessori teachers must serve a year's internship under an experienced Montessori teacher before they can be accredited, there are more student-teachers available for Montessori classes than might be true for other situations. The alternatives are operating without an assistant or taking more children into the class where there is to be an assistant. Although not ideal, either might work out reasonably well in any given situation. The fact that Montessori's first Casa dei Bambini began with over fifty children and only one untrained teacher is sometimes overlooked.

Third, Montessori equipment is so attractive and well made that it looks far more expensive than it is. It costs approximately $1,000 for a set of materials for thirty children aged three to six. This is close to the cost of setting up a traditional nursery school today with its expensive indoor jungle-gyms, rocking boats, wooden refrigerators and stoves, kitchen utensils, doll houses, dolls, doll clothes, dress-up corner, puzzles, etc. Moreover, Montessori equipment does not have to be constantly replaced and repaired, as the equipment in most nursery schools and traditional classrooms does, because it is so meticulously constructed and because the children are taught to handle it with care. Montessori materials for children of six to twelve do not come in ordered sets as the introductory material does. The teacher makes a selection to suit her children's needs from a catalogue of many materials. Whatever her selection, $1,000 to $1,500 will completely equip a classroom for thirty to thirty-five children in the six-to-twelve-year age range. This does represent an initial outlay well beyond what most public schools spend today on their grade school and junior high school classes. However, it should be remembered that this is a capital expense, and not subject to frequent recurrence as are the costs of readers, textbooks, science kits, etc. It is an expense also well below that of the talking typewriters, computers, television sets, etc. (and their repair) now being advocated as an answer to the educational problems of inner-city schools.

Having discussed the expense of the Montessori materials, their relative importance to the method should also be considered. It is quite possible to produce a top-quality Montessori classroom without any of the manufactured Montessori materials. In fact, for many teachers, particularly those who have been teaching a good many years and are likely to be set in their ways, it would be better for them to prepare their own materials. In this way, they must carefully think through how they are going to use the materials to further the deeper aims of Montessori education.

When a teacher is presented with the Montessori materials as a whole, there is a danger she may regard them in the old way, i.e., as a set curriculum which the child must be rigidly marched through, instead of as a means whereby he can achieve independence, self-discipline, and creativity. There are classrooms where this has happened, and visitors there have imagined they were seeing a Montessori classroom. Nothing could be further from the truth. It is the teacher's attitude toward the children and herself that establishes a Montessori classroom. If, in addition to this attitude, the teacher has access to Montessori materials—all well and good—but, if not, she can adapt the educational equipment she does have available to her, or she can develop her own. There are today many educational tools that, with a few adjustments, can meet the standards and principles Montessori established for her materials, and completely new equipment can be developed out of relatively inexpensive materials as well. Some very good equipment would undoubtedly be created in this way, and it is an approach very much in keeping with Montessori's own experimental outlook.

Although operating costs are not necessarily higher for Montessori education, there will be some initial expenses for any classrooms that are begun, either for retraining teachers or for purchasing or developing materials. Because they do want a better education for their children, I believe parents themselves would work to raise the needed funds. Undertaken classroom by classroom, it is not such an insurmountable task, and "parent power" can be a formidable force. The one thousand or so existing Montessori schools in this country were virtually all started through the energy, resources, and influence of parents.

It may be that parents are rejecting school bond issues today in part because they reject the type of education their children are receiving. They may not want more of the same. School boards might well consider giving them something to vote for, instead of something to vote against. They might offer them this highly innovative, highly visual, and easily understood method of education which their children will, for a change, enjoy. The response might surprise them. (I am reminded of a nine-year-old friend of mine who, when I asked her what she would do if she were allowed to do whatever she wanted in school, replied, "Leave!" Who in this day and age wants to spend more money to continue an educational experience their children feel that way about?)

Montessori education is not a panacea for the problems of our society today, as some enthusiasts might have us believe. Because human beings must accomplish it, it is always exceedingly difficult to reproduce quality classrooms of any educational method on a large scale. Montessori is no exception. In addition, Montessori education represents primarily the genius of one person who developed educational practices based on an approach to children that had never been tried successfully before. It is therefore a pioneering effort, and should not be regarded as the final answer to this approach. Other equally effective methods may be developed in the future based on the same approach to the child. Montessori philosophy and method then deserve credit as a beginning— the first real beginning—to seeking the answers to the child's education and life out of *his* experiences and not out of our own. As such, they represent an excellent foundation on which to build the education of the future.

Appendix:
Research Results

UNTIL 1964, no scientifically designed research study in Montessori education had been undertaken. In that year a group of parents in Cincinnati began to develop such a program. They felt it was essential to have documented proof of the successes they thought they saw in the classroom if Montessori was to move from its historical position on the fringes of the educational scene and enter the mainstream. They made the necessary arrangements for establishing three new Montessori classes, obtained Office of Economic Opportunity funds to finance them, interested the Department of Psychology at the University of Cincinnati in organizing a research team, and raised approximately $100,000 from local foundations to cover research expenses. The research design was to cover a three-year period, with a follow-up study to be done in the sixth year, when the original subjects were expected to be in the third grade. The study became operative in 1965 and was known as the Cincinnati Montessori Research Project. Dr. Thomas Banta, of the Department of Psychology, University of Cincinnati, was selected as the Project Director.

After the initial pre-testing and selection of approximately 150 children for the Montessori, comparative, and control classes were completed, the research team began the task of developing tests to use in evaluating the results of the educational experiences of the children. It was felt that the tests in use to determine intelligence of young children, such as the Stanford Binet or the Peabody Picture Vocabulary, would be inadequate as the sole measures in the study. These tests, designed to measure appropriate, conventional, and quick responses, would not indicate the development of other abilities more pertinent to Montessori education. The tests developed became known as the Cincinnati Autonomy Test Battery. "Autonomy" was considered as "self-regulating behaviors that facilitate effective problem-solving." This meant that various strengths of the child would have to be measured. Fourteen variables were selected to assess the following behaviors: curiosity and assertiveness, exploratory behavior, creativity, innovative behavior, motor impulse control, attention, persistence, reflectivity, field independence, and analytic perceptual processes. The tests were carefully designed not to favor Montessori methods, nor were any materials used that Montessori children would find more familiar than other children.

In the three years of testing, the Montessori children scored consistently highest or next to highest on all variables. Because the results were based on tests whose reliability is not yet sufficiently established, and because the results were not always statistically significant, they cannot be acclaimed as proof of Montessori superiority. On the other hand, they were sufficiently promising to encourage those who had organized the project to extend it for another three years, instead of being satisfied with a follow-up study in the sixth year, as originally intended. With the cooperation of the Cincinnati Board of Education and the Carnegie Corporation of New York, which funded the research component and a good portion of the classroom expenses, the Sands School Montessori Class and several control classes were established. The Sands School Montessori Class represented a continuation of the Montessori approach into a first-grade, public school setting for approximately twenty-five children from Montessori Head Start classes in several parts of the city. All of the children were original subjects in the research program, so that by 1970 they would have been followed by research through six continuous years of Montessori education, from the ages of three to nine. The major thrust of the evaluation for the second three-year period was to be the comparison of performance of four groups of children: (1) the Montessori classroom, (2) a non-graded classroom, (3) children with pre-school experience and in conventional (graded) classrooms, and (4) children without pre-school experience and in conventional (graded) classrooms.

Dr. Banta served as Project Director in the first year of the newly organized project. In the second year, Dr. Ruth Gross of the Department of Psychiatry, College of Medicine, University of Cincinnati, took over as Project Director while Dr. Banta was on academic leave.

In the first and second years, Dr. Banta's Cincinnati Autonomy Test Battery was again used for evaluation, with some other measures added the second year by Dr. Gross. Again the Montessori children scored highest or next to highest on all measures used in this two-year testing period. Although it should be restated the reliability of some of the tests used has still to be proven, the research team found these results "a very promising finding for the Montessori Method."

An additional test, the Metropolitan Readiness Tests, was given in the first year of the study by the Cincinnati Public Schools. According to the manual of this test, it was "devised to measure the extent to which school beginners have developed in the several skills and abilities that contribute to readiness for first-grade instruction." Bonnie Green, a Research Associate in the Department of Psychiatry, College of Medicine, University of Cincinnati, and a member of the research team, analyzed the results of this test: "In conclusion, at the end of kindergarten, it was demonstrated that the Montessori class was most mature and ready for first-grade instruction, as defined by the Metropolitan Readiness Tests, and the control class without pre-school was least ready, with non-graded class and the control class with pre-school being second and third." The results were considered statistically significant.

In the third year, research was shifted from testing of specific variables to an interview approach which, while not providing the scientific data of earlier procedures, did provide an opportunity for answering certain subjective questions. Three studies were done: one involved interviews with forty children, ten randomly selected from each of the four original groups; a second, interviews with a selected number of mothers representing each of the four groups of children; and a third, interviews with a number of Montessori and non-graded teachers from the community, including a number of Sands teachers and two administrators. Three findings were of particular significance:

First, the third-year Sands School Project Report states that "The Montessori children as a group appeared much more extroverted, verbal, and personable than the other three groups of children. They had more to say, could express it better, and had fewer articulation problems than the other children. The Montessori children's advanced ability to communicate, therefore, made them appear more socially confident, assured, and at ease in adult company than the other groups."

Second, "Montessori parents appeared more verbal in general than those from other groups and more knowledgeable about teaching objectives." Because of the way in which the children were selected for the classes, the researchers felt it unlikely the parents had been more verbal and aware of educative processes before their children entered Montessori. It is reasonable to assume that the close contact with parents which is an integral part of the Montessori method had had some impact on the parents, and that it would be a worthwhile area to pursue in further research.

Third, "While other teachers expressed a concern for individual development of potentialities, Montessori teachers appeared to have more experience and sophistication in individualization of learning. If conventional education accepts individualized learning as a positive value, this may be where Montessori as an approach can enter the mainstream of education."

A new research program is being developed to pursue further the areas suggested by the results of the past six years of research study, and in particular to describe the actual processes going on in the Montessori classroom itself. At present the research team, now under the direction of Dr. June Scirra, is examining the earliest test scores from the first year of testing in order to relate them to grade-school performance. This long-term follow-up study is the first systematic effort to assess objectively the lasting effects of Montessori in comparison with other educational procedures.

Copies of research reports covering the years 1965–68 can be obtained by writing to Dr. Thomas Banta, Department of Psychology, University of Cincinnati. Requests for reports for the years 1968–70 should be directed to Dr. Ruth Gross, Department of Psychiatry, College of Medicine, University of Cincinnati; and for the six-year follow-up study to be completed in 1971, to Dr. June Scirra, Child Development Center, University of Cincinnati.

Notes

PREFACE

1. Dorothy Canfield Fisher, *The Montessori Mother*, pp. xiv–xvi.
2. E. M. Standing, *Maria Montessori: Her Life and Work*, p. 59.

CHAPTER 1

1. Standing, *op. cit.*, p. 11.
2. Montessori, *The Montessori Method*, pp. 38–39.
3. *Ibid.*, p. 33.
4. *Ibid.*, p. 41.
5. Montessori, *The Secret of Childhood*, p. 129.
6. *Ibid.*, p. 114.
7. *Ibid.*, p. 129.
8. *Ibid.*, p. 133.
9. *Ibid.*, p. 134.
10. *Ibid.*, p. 156.
11. Montessori, *The Discovery of the Child*, p. vi.
12. William Kilpatrick, *The Montessori System Examined*, pp. vii–ix.
13. *Ibid.*, p. 62.
14. *Ibid.*, pp. 62–63.
15. *Ibid.*, p. 41.
16. *Ibid.*, p. 20.
17. *Ibid.*, pp. 15–16.
18. *Ibid.*, p. 20.

19. *Ibid.*, pp. 27–28.
20. *Ibid.*, pp. 28–29.
21. *Ibid.*, pp. 34–35.
22. *Ibid.*, p. 42.
23. *Ibid.*, p. 45.
24. *Ibid.*, pp. 49–50.
25. *Ibid.*, p. 52.
26. *Ibid.*, pp. 47–48.
27. *Ibid.*, pp. 21–22.
28. *Ibid.*, pp. 58–59.
29. *Ibid.*, p. 55.
30. *Ibid.*, p. 58.
31. *Ibid.*, p. 60.
32. *Ibid.*, p. 40.
33. *Ibid.*, pp. 63–64.
34. *Ibid.*, pp. 65–66.
35. Montessori, *Spontaneous Activity in Education*, p. 64.
36. Montessori, *What You Should Know About Your Child*, p. 130.
37. H. F. Harlow, "Mice, Monkeys, Men and Motives," pp. 29–30.
38. J. McV. Hunt, "The Epigenesis of Motivation and Early Cognitive Learning," p. 365.
39. *Ibid.*, p. 366.
40. Jean Piaget, *The Psychology of Intelligence*, p. 119.
41. Jean Piaget and Barbel Inhelder, *The Psychology of the Child*, p. 5.
42. Piaget, *op. cit.*, p. 123.
43. Piaget and Inhelder, *op. cit.*, p. 153.
44. For other experiments, *see* Donald W. Fiske and Salvatore R. Maddi, *Functions of Varied Experience*.
45. Piaget and Inhelder, *op. cit.*, p. 13.
46. *Ibid.*, p. 149.
47. Piaget, *op. cit.*, pp. 150–51.
48. Rudolf Arnheim, *Visual Thinking*, pp. v, 264.
49. *Ibid.*, p. 13.
50. *Ibid.*, p. 205.
51. *Ibid.*, pp. 300–301.

CHAPTER 2

1. Standing, *op. cit.*, p. 348.
2. Montessori, *The Child in the Church*, p. 7.
3. *Ibid.*, pp. 9, 7.
4. *The Discovery of the Child*, p. xiv.
5. *What You Should Know About Your Child*, p. 25.
6. Montessori, *The Absorbent Mind*, p. 140.
7. *The Secret of Childhood*, p. 103.
8. *The Absorbent Mind*, p. 86.
9. *Ibid.*, p. 146.
10. *Ibid.*, p. 147.
11. *Ibid.*, p. 83.
12. *Ibid.*, p. 97.
13. *The Secret of Childhood*, p. 44.
14. *Ibid.*, p. 58.
15. *Ibid.*, p. 87.
16. *Ibid.*
17. *Ibid.*, p. 82.
18. *Ibid.*, p. 207.
19. *The Absorbent Mind*, p. 25.
20. *Ibid.*, p. 117.
21. *What You Should Know About Your Child*, p. 54.
22. *The Absorbent Mind*, p. 165.
23. *The Secret of Childhood*, p. 208.
24. *The Absorbent Mind*, p. 92.
25. *The Secret of Childhood*, p. 212.
26. *Ibid.*, p. 211.
27. *The Absorbent Mind*, p. 85.
28. *Ibid.*, p. 217.
29. *Ibid.*, p. 206.
30. Montessori, *Education for a New World*, p. 71.
31. *The Absorbent Mind*, p. 254.
32. *Ibid.*, p. 255.
33. *What You Should Know About Your Child*, p. 73.
34. *Ibid.*, p. 84.
35. *The Absorbent Mind*, p. 257.
36. *Ibid.*, pp. 252–54.
37. *Ibid.*, pp. 256–57.
38. *Ibid.*, p. 257.

39. *Ibid.*
40. *Ibid.,* p. 253.
41. George Dennison, *The Lives of Children,* pp. 112–13.
42. *Spontaneous Activity in Education,* p. 195.
43. *Ibid.,* p. 198.
44. *Ibid.,* p. 202.
45. *Ibid.,* p. 212.
46. *Ibid.,* p. 257.
47. *The Absorbent Mind,* pp. 254–55.
48. *See* Arthur Koestler's stimulating book *The Act of Creation,* for an excellent description of the creative process which encompasses Montessori's own approach.
49. *Spontaneous Activity in Education,* p. 335.
50. *Ibid.,* p. 337.
51. *Ibid.,* p. 340.
52. *Education for a New World,* pp. 2–3.

CHAPTER 3

1. *The Montessori Method,* p. 105.
2. *Ibid.*
3. *The Secret of Childhood,* p. 224.
4. *The Montessori Method,* p. 28.
5. *Ibid.,* p. 15.
6. *The Absorbent Mind,* p. 205.
7. *The Secret of Childhood,* p. 207.
8. *The Montessori Method,* pp. 95–98.
9. *Education for a New World,* p. 79.
10. *The Montessori Method,* p. 93.
11. *Ibid.,* p. 87.
12. *Ibid.,* p. 93.
13. *Ibid.,* p. 87.
14. *Ibid.,* pp. 80–81.
15. *Ibid.,* p. 88.
16. *Ibid.*
17. *Spontaneous Activity in Education,* p. 70.
18. *Ibid.,* p. 43.
19. *The Montessori Method,* p. 21.
20. *The Absorbent Mind,* pp. 223–24.
21. *Ibid.,* p. 224.
22. *The Absorbent Mind,* p. 223.

23. *The Montessori Method*, p. 153.
24. *Ibid.*, p. 155.
25. *What You Should Know About Your Child*, p. 105.
26. *The Montessori Method*, p. 171.
27. *The Absorbent Mind*, p. 221.
28. *Spontaneous Activity in Education*, p. 81.
29. *Ibid.*, pp. 73–74.
30. *Ibid.*, pp. 77–79.
31. *Ibid.*, pp. 73–74.
32. *Ibid.*, p. 81.
33. *Ibid.*, p. 77.
34. *Ibid.*
35. *The Absorbent Mind*, p. 248.
36. *Spontaneous Activity in Education*, p. 75.
37. *Ibid.*, p. 76.
38. *The Montessori Method*, p. 107.
39. *Ibid.*, p. 115.
40. *Ibid.*, pp. 107–8.
41. *Spontaneous Activity in Education*, p. 43.
42. *The Absorbent Mind*, p. 179.
43. *Ibid.*, p. 108.
44. *Ibid.*
45. *Ibid.*, pp. 108–9.
46. *Ibid.*, pp. 357–58.
47. John and Evelyn Dewey, *Schools of Tomorrow*, pp. 157–58.
48. *The Montessori Method*, p. 225.
49. *Ibid.*, p. 226.
50. *Ibid.*, p. 227.
51. *What You Should Know About Your Child*, p. 114.
52. *The Montessori Method*, p. 360.
53. *The Discovery of the Child*, p. 345.
54. *The Montessori Method*, pp. 162–66.
55. *Spontaneous Activity in Education*, p. 311.
56. *Ibid.*
57. *The Absorbent Mind*, p. 229.
58. *Ibid.*, pp. 225–26.
59. *Ibid.*, p. 228.
60. *Ibid.*, p. 226.
61. *Ibid.*, p. 227.
62. *The Montessori Method*, p. 93.
63. *Ibid.*, p. 94.

64. *Ibid.*, p. 210.
65. *Ibid.*, p. 211.
66. *The Absorbent Mind*, p. 132.
67. *The Secret of Childhood*, p. 115.
68. *Ibid.*, p. 11.
69. *Ibid.*, p. 12.
70. *Ibid.*, pp. 79–80.
71. *Spontaneous Activity in Education*, p. 130.
72. *The Montessori Method*, p. 87.
73. *Ibid.*, p. 88.
74. *Spontaneous Activity in Education*, pp. 130–31.
75. *The Montessori Method*, p. 9.
76. *Ibid.*, p. 12.
77. *Ibid.*, p. 104.
78. *Ibid.*, p. 13.
79. *Spontaneous Activity in Education*, p. 122.
80. *Ibid.*, pp. 122–24.
81. *The Absorbent Mind*, p. 278.
82. *Ibid.*
83. *Ibid.*
84. *Ibid.*, p. 246.
85. *Ibid.*, pp. 248–49.
86. *Ibid.*, p. 134.
87. *The Montessori Method*, pp. 37–38.
88. *The Secret of Childhood*, pp. 96–97.
89. *The Montessori Method*, p. 61.
90. *Ibid.*
91. *Ibid.*, pp. 61–62.
92. *Ibid.*, pp. 63–64.
93. *Ibid.*, p. 64
94. *The Absorbent Mind*, p. 263.
95. *Ibid.*, p. 264.
96. *Ibid.*, pp. 268–69.
97. *Ibid.*, p. 279.
98. *Ibid.*, pp. 279–80.
99. *Ibid.*, p. 270.
100. *Ibid.*, p. 274.
101. *Ibid.*, p. 275.
102. *Ibid.*
103. *Ibid.*, p. 281.
104. *Ibid.*

CHAPTER 4

1. *The Secret of Childhood*, pp. 248–49.
2. *Ibid.*, p. 249.
3. *Ibid.*, pp. 233–34.
4. *Ibid.*, p. 234.
5. *What You Should Know About Your Child*, pp. 26–27.
6. *The Absorbent Mind*, p. 99.
7. *The Secret of Childhood*, p. 18.
8. *The Absorbent Mind*, pp. 100–101.
9. *The Secret of Childhood*, p. 179.
10. *The Montessori Method*, p. 69.
11. *The Secret of Childhood*, p. 263.
12. *The Absorbent Mind*, pp. 14–15.
13. *Ibid.*, p. 103.
14. Montessori, *Reconstruction in Education*, pp. 4–5.
15. Erik Erikson, *Childhood and Society*, p. 69.
16. *The Secret of Childhood*, pp. 93–94.
17. Fisher, *The Montessori Mother*, p. 24.
18. *The Secret of Childhood*, p. 99.
19. *Ibid.*, pp. 235–36.
20. *The Absorbent Mind*, pp. 103–4.
21. *Ibid.*, p. 100.
22. *The Absorbent Mind*, pp. 104–5.
23. *Ibid.*, p. 106.
24. *Ibid.*, p. 109.
25. *The Secret of Childhood*, p. 74.
26. *Spontaneous Activity in Education*, p. 297.
27. *The Secret of Childhood*, pp. 81–82.
28. *Ibid.*, p. 86.
29. *Ibid.*, p. 87–88.
30. *Ibid.*, p. 90.
31. *Ibid.*
32. *What You Should Know About Your Child*, p. 12.
33. *The Montessori Method*, pp. 96–99.
34. *Ibid.*, p. 100.
35. *The Absorbent Mind*, p. 93.
36. *What You Should Know About Your Child*, p. 131.
37. Erikson, *op. cit.*, pp. 235–36.
38. *Education for a New World*, p. 64.

39. *The Secret of Childhood*, p. 173.

40. *Ibid.*, pp. 91–92.

41. *Ibid.*, p. 92.

42. *Education for a New World*, p. 64.

43. *Ibid.*, p. 65.

44. *What You Should Know About Your Child*, p. 73.

45. *Reconstruction in Education*, p. 10.

46. *See* Virginia M. Axline, *Dibs in Search of Self* (New York: Ballantine Books, 1969), an excellent book for all adults who work with children.

47. *What You Should Know About Your Child*, p. 131.

CHAPTER 5

1. *Dr. Montessori's Own Handbook*, p. 134.

CHAPTER 6

1. *What You Should Know About Your Child*, p. 132.

2. *The Montessori Method*, p. 155.

3. *The Discovery of the Child*, p. 99.

4. *Ibid.*, p. 98.

5. For further information, write to Minnesota Outward Bound School, 330 Walker Avenue, Wayzata, Minnesota 55391.

Bibliography

Arnheim, Rudolf. *Visual Thinking*. London: Faber & Faber; Berkeley: University of California Press, 1969.

Association Montessori Internationale. *Maria Montessori, A Centenary Anthology*. Amsterdam, 1970.

Bruner, Jerome S., *et al. Studies in Cognitive Growth*. New York: John Wiley & Sons, 1966.

Dennison, George. *The Lives of Children*. New York: Random House, 1969.

Dewey, John and Evelyn. *Schools of Tomorrow*. New York: E. P. Dutton, 1915.

Elkins, David, "Piaget and Montessori," *Harvard Educational Review*, XXXVII (1967), 535–46.

Erikson, Erik H. *Childhood and Society*. New York: W. W. Norton, 1940.

Fisher, Dorothy Canfield. *Montessori for Parents*. Cambridge, Mass.: Robert Bentley, Inc., 1965.

————. *The Montessori Mother*. London: Constable, 1913.

Fiske, Donald W., and Maddi, Salvatore R. *Functions of Varied Experience*. Homewood, Ill.: Dorsey Press, 1961.

Harlow, H. F. "Mice, Monkeys, Men and Motives," *Psychology Review*, LX (1953), 23–32.

Hebb, Donald O. "Drives and the C.N.S.," in *Current Research in Motivation*, ed. Ralph Norman Haber, pp. 267–78. New York: Holt, Rinehart & Winston, 1966.

————. *Organization of Behavior*. New York: John Wiley & Sons, 1949.

Hess, Eckhard. "Ethology and Developmental Psychology," in *Carmichael's Manual of Child Psychology*, ed. Paul Mussen, pp. 1–33. New York: John Wiley & Sons, 1970.

Holt, John. *How Children Fail.* New York: Pitman, 1964.

Hunt, J. McV. "The Epigenesis of Motivation and Early Cognitive Learning," in *Current Research in Motivation*, ed. Ralph Norman Haber, pp. 355–70. New York: Holt, Rinehart & Winston, 1966.

———. *Intelligence and Experience.* New York: Ronald Press, 1961.

Itard, Jean. *Wild Boy of Aveyron.* New York: Appleton-Century-Crofts, 1962.

Kagan, Jerome, and Kogan, Nathan. "Individuality and Cognitive Performance," in *Carmichael's Manual of Child Psychology*, ed. Paul Mussen, pp. 1273–1353. New York: John Wiley & Sons, 1970.

Kilpatrick, William. *The Montessori System Examined.* Boston: Houghton Mifflin, 1914.

Koestler, Arthur. *The Act of Creation.* New York: Macmillan, 1964.

Lillard, Paula P. *A Montessori Study Guide.* New York: American Montessori Society, 1970.

Montessori, Maria. *The Absorbent Mind.* Wheaton, Ill.: Theosophical Press, 1964.

———. *The Child in the Church*, ed. E. M. Standing. St. Paul, Minn.: Catechetical Guild, 1965.

———. *The Discovery of the Child.* Wheaton, Ill.: Theosophical Press, 1962.

———. *Dr. Montessori's Own Handbook.* New York: Schocken Books, 1965.

———. *Education for a New World.* Wheaton, Ill.: Theosophical Press, 1963.

———. *The Formation of Man.* Wheaton, Ill.: Theosophical Press, 1969.

———. *The Montessori Method.* New York: Schocken Books, 1964.

———. *Reconstruction in Education.* Wheaton, Ill.: Theosophical Press, 1964.

———. *The Secret of Childhood.* Calcutta: Orient Longmans, Ltd., 1963.

———. *Spontaneous Activity in Education.* New York: Schocken Books, 1965.

———. *To Educate the Human Potential.* Wheaton, Ill.: Theosophical Press, 1963.

————. *What You Should Know About Your Child*. Wheaton, Ill.: Theosophical Press, 1963.

Piaget, Jean. *The Psychology of Intelligence*. Totowa, N.J.: Littlefield, Adams, 1963.

————, and Inhelder, Barbel. *The Psychology of the Child*. Translated from the French by Helen Weaver. New York: Basic Books, 1969.

Rambusch, Nancy McCormick. *Learning How to Learn*. Baltimore: Helicon Press, 1962.

Séguin, Edouard. *Idiocy and Its Treatment*. Albany, N.Y.: Press of Brandow Printing Co., 1907.

Spitz, R. A. "Hospitalism: An Inquiry into the Genesis of Psychiatric Conditions in Early Childhood," in *The Psychoanalytic Study of the Child*, I, pp. 53–74. New York: International Universities Press, 1945.

Standing, E. M. *Maria Montessori: Her Life and Work*. Fresno, Calif.: Academy Guild Press, 1959.

————. *The Montessori Revolution in Education*. New York: Schocken Books, 1966.

White, Jessie. *Montessori Schools*. London: Oxford University Press, 1914

SUGGESTED READING IN CONTEMPORARY EDUCATION

Axline, Virginia M. *Dibs in Search of Self*. New York: Ballantine Books, 1969.

Dennison, George. *The Lives of Children*. New York: Random House, 1969.

Ginott, Haim. *Between Parent and Child*. New York: Macmillan, 1967.

Holt, John. *How Children Fail*. New York: Pitman, 1964.

————. *How Children Learn*. New York: Pitman, 1967.

————. *The Underachieving School*. New York: Pitman, 1969.

————. *What Do I Do Monday?* New York: E. P. Dutton, 1970.

Kohl, Herbert. *The Open Classroom*. New York Review Press, 1969.

Leonard, George. *Education and Ecstasy*. New York: Delacorte, 1968.

Silberman, Charles. *Crisis in the Classroom*. New York: Random House, 1970.

Index

171